THE HEART

OF THE

Goddess

THE HEART

OF THE

Goddess

ART, MYTH AND MEDITATIONS OF THE
WORLD'S SACRED FEMININE

HALLIE IGLEHART AUSTEN

Wingbow Press
Berkeley

Cover and text design: Brenn Lea Pearson, San Francisco
Typesetting: Execustaff, Campbell, California
Printing: Snow Lion Graphics, Berkeley, Hong Kong

Special thanks for the cover images to the following:
Shalako Mana: Photo courtesy of the Museum of the American
Indian, Heye Foundation, New York
Gabon Ancestor Mask: Photo courtesy of the Museum voor
Volkenkunde, Rotterdam
Artemis: Photo courtesy of Giroudon/Art Resource, New York,
Musée du Louvre, Paris
Hine-titama: Courtesy of Robyn Kahukiwa

The author and the publisher have arranged that two trees are
planted in a Costa Rican rain forest for every tree needed
to manufacture the paper for this book. See Resources on
page 171 for further information on Arbofilia.

First Edition: October, 1990
Second Printing: August, 1991

ISBN 0-914728-69-5

Wingbow Press books are published and distributed by
Bookpeople, 7900 Edgewater Drive, Oakland, California 94621

To the renewal of Gaia,
our Mother,
and to the Goddess
in every being.

CONTENTS

THE HEART OF THE GODDESS

ACKNOWLEDGMENTS

A book of this scope could never be the work of only one person. I am indebted to a number of people and I trust that the merit of their efforts will return to them many times over. I would like to thank them in the chronological order of their influence on this book.

Sandra Roos first inspired me with the visual beauty of the Goddess and encouraged me to put together my own slideshow, from which this book evolved. Karen Vogel was a partner in expanding the slideshow and in the conception of the book, whose early vision she helped shape.

My sister-in-law, Lily Lopez Iglehart, spent a month with me cataloguing the permissions information for each image—such friendship and assistance were invaluable. My assistant, Stephanie Houston, helped with infinite details at every stage of the project. She also compiled the bibliography, massaged my shoulders and buoyed my spirit with her cheerful encouragement. Gina Banghart volunteered a winter season to help with the research and offered me much-appreciated spiritual support.

Lynne Dal Poggetto miraculously obtained permissions from sources all over the world to reproduce these images. Lynne supplied me with several visual gems and was a constant ally in the project. A number of gems were also unearthed by Joan Iten Sutherland. I can never thank Joan enough for her scholarship, editing, translating (Chinese and Japanese), and creative input. I am proud to be part of a growing list of authors who have relied on Joan's and Lynne's expertise and moral support.

Vicki Noble provided great support with her valuable knowledge and insights on each Goddess. Both Vicki and Karen Vogel loaned me parts of their extensive libraries, for which I am most grateful.

My editor, Randy Fingland of Wingbow Press, has demonstrated all the best qualities of an editor. In particular, I thank him for his rare degree of patience, thoroughness and perception. My thanks to all at Wingbow for their fine work. I feel very fortunate that Brenn Lea Pearson was the designer of this book. She has performed the magic of bringing to life my vision of it.

I am grateful to Asungi, Arisika Razak and Roslyn Adele Walker, assistant curator at the National Museum of African Art, Smithsonian Institution, for reviewing the African material; to Paula Gunn Allen, Professor of Native American Studies at the University of California, Berkeley, and Sacheen (Cruz) Littlefeather for feedback on the Native American sections; to Nancy Hock, curator of Southeast Asian Art at the Asian Art Museum of San Francisco for going over the East Asian text; and to Joan Sutherland for her knowledge of Asian and Old European cultures. I hasten to add that none of the above is responsible for my interpretations or for any inaccuracies that may appear in this work.

My parents, Harriet Austen Stokes Iglehart and Francis Nash Iglehart, raised me with a fine sense of the power of myth and of the beauty of the earth. I am more grateful than I can say for their sensitivity and their support throughout the years.

I would also like to thank Deborah Anne Light for her belief in me and in this project. Deep appreciation to Linda Evans for emotional sustenance and editing advice and to Marcelina Martin for her support and assistance.

There are many dear friends, neighbors and associates who have helped sustain me and/or offered their particular expertise: Ruth Eckland, Barbara Lakshmi Kahn, Riitta Leitso, Arisika Razak, Nancy Stein and Patrice Wynne. This list could be nearly endless, and I must stop here and say to those who have helped make this book possible—deepest gratitude and many blessings to you and to all who have helped ease the rebirth of the Sacred Feminine.

A constant source of inspiration and energy for me has been the land and wild inhabitants, seen and unseen, of the Point Reyes area. May you be protected. And may the beings of all lands benefit from this work and from the prayers and actions of all who know it.

Hallie Iglehart Austen
Point Reyes
Winter Solstice 1989

FOREWORD

The Goddess reveals many aspects of herself in Hallie Iglehart Austen's magnificently conceived book. The reader becomes an Initiate into the feminine mysteries if the images and words within these pages are felt and known inwardly, illuminating the hidden, obvious truth: "Of course—the Creator and Comforter would have a feminine form."

The author, whose previous book *Womanspirit* was a significant contribution to women's spirituality, has now assembled and organized a major collection of images of the sacred feminine. She writes of the Goddesses with the ease of someone who knows them well, and in introducing them, she provides us with a sketch of the historical, archeological, mythological, and anthropological context in which they existed or were found.

But Austen's book does more than provide us with information, it offers the possibility of having a subjective experience. There is a priestess in this author, whose arrangement and progression of the Goddesses is an enactment of ritual invocation that takes us from Creation to Transformation and then to Celebration. Her inclusion and choice of chants, poetry and ritual invites us to hear words, feel the cadence, respond with feelings and imagination, and thus shift out of the objective realm into a liminal one.

As archetypal images, Goddesses have the potential to be experienced inwardly to begin with, which is then enhanced by the accompanying text. The consequence of becoming subjectively aware of the Goddess or being touched by her in any of her forms is great, for—as Starhawk's chant says—"She changes everything she touches and everything she touches, changes."

This idea, however heretical it is to Judeo-Christian and Islamic traditionalists, is just the beginning of insight into the mysterious nature of the Goddess and the presence of the Goddess in women. That divinity and psyche have a feminine aspect that is deeply sacred, awesome and embodied rings true archetypally. This is knowledge that we have within us, part of the collective unconscious that we all share. It is knowledge that has been repressed by patriarchal religions, which has stressed that men rule by divine right, and have dominion over the Earth and over women who—unlike men—were said not to have been made in the image of God. The images in *The Heart of the Goddess* belie what we are still told about the exclusively masculine nature of the deity.

As the author of *Goddesses in Everywoman*, I did extensive research into goddess mythology, which makes me very aware that this book has the potential to become a major source of information. But I see that the potential of this book to initiate and change women and some exceptional men is its greater potential. The woman who absorbs the images as she looks at the photographs and understands the implications of what she is reading, or hears the poetry and chants and uses her imagination, or enacts rituals and feels something shift within herself, usually finds that her dream life, indeed her whole life, is affected, for she is changing from within and is taking in and taking on an awareness of the sacredness and strength in women through meeting the Goddesses.

In preparation for writing this Foreword, I dismantled the manuscript and covered my entire living room floor with the color copies of the photographs that appear in the book. I gazed around me at the lot of them, as well as picking them up one at a time to take each one in individually. I found that they were either immediately charismatic or they grew on me. Most of us have been brought up to be ashamed of our bodies and our genitals, and the dominant culture values only youthful, slender (and usually Caucasian) figures as beautiful. But as I lived with the images of this book, what was strange became familiar, those that were initially off-putting to me became beautiful in their own way or awesome, worthy of respect and acceptance.

Certainly there is a destructive aspect to the feminine, in women as well as in Goddesses, just as in the natural world, decay and death are necessary parts of the process of regeneration. Unless we know and respect this complexity that the Transformative Goddesses represent (that which is undeveloped or repressed or rejected), we are split off and separated from what they are in ourselves: earthiness, lustiness, sexuality, power, ecstasy, death.

We cannot encounter the Goddess without women, for the Goddess either has the form of a woman (when she is seen in a vision or represented by a sculpture or painting, for example) or she is experienced through a woman. It is in a woman's arms, for instance, that we may meet the Mother Goddess or the Goddess of Love. Even when feminine qualities are deified and abstracted as life-giving or life-sustaining, they are still embodied. When the planet Earth is revered as Gaia, for example, this is not just an idea or just a spirit, but the presence of the Goddess in living matter.

Since Goddesses and women share attributes, to look upon the many images of the Goddess contained in *The Heart of the Goddess* is both to see her myriad forms, and for women, to see reflections of themselves in her.

To be moved by these images is to be part of what I have long been calling "the last wave of the women's movement", otherwise called "women's spirituality". It is the acceptance of women's experience as sacred, as spiritual, and whatever women do to honor what they know, as ritual.

This book is an invocation of the Goddess.

Jean Shinoda Bolen, M.D.

INTRODUCTION

The Goddess and Sacred Feminine, embodiment and reassurance of the possibility of a beneficent universe, are reawakening in the hearts and minds of peoples throughout the world. This re-emergence coincides with the growth of other movements which affirm the interconnectedness and sanctity of life. Members of the peace, environmental, feminist, human and gay rights and earth religion movements find guidance and inspiration in contemplating the images, traditions and values of Gaia, Spider Grandmother, Tara, Ochun, Kali and Guanyin, to name only a few aspects of the worldwide Goddess.

Goddess of Democracy. Tiananmen Square, Beijing, China, 1989. Photo by Tsao Hsingyuan.

background material and meditations of this book will help readers contribute to rediscovering the true nature of the Sacred Feminine.

For many years, I began my classes on women's spirituality by showing slides of both ancient and contemporary Goddess art. Seeing these images served to ground my students in the prehistorical and historical reality of societies in which women and women's wisdom were central to everyday life. I found myself and others profoundly moved and healed by looking at these pictures. No matter what my previous mood, I always felt stronger and more peaceful after seeing the Goddesses.

The impetus for this book comes from my great love for the Sacred Feminine and for these images in particular. As I see it, the knowledge and direct experience of the Great Goddess, once revered throughout the world, has been lost, obscured by patriarchal repression and distortion. Different aspects of the original Great Goddess have survived in various cultures and deities. We must look to all of them in order to find out who the Goddess really is. My hope is that the images,

THE SACRED ART

Images have an enormous influence on us, as evidenced by the mass of visual media and advertising in our culture. In order to free our psyches, we must carefully chose our images and the messages they convey. Pictures speak to our hearts and our guts, as well as to our minds. In addition, it is harder to obscure the message of an image. As we have seen in feminist and other contemporary analyses of history and religion, words can be mistranslated, either deliberately or as a result of cultural prejudice or political manipulation. Pictures, however, speak directly to us.

In preparing this book I had two primary criteria for choosing images: visual impact and cross-cultural perspective. Of course, limitations of time, money and accessibility have also been determining factors. For example, I have found hardly any Goddess art from South America, as little archeological research has been done there. However, we have many riches from Central America and we know that the famous Machu Picchu complex in Peru was a temple for priestesses.

There are many important Goddesses and revealing works of Goddess art which I have not included, as I sought, among the images available to me, those best able to convey the broad range of the Goddess's beauty, power and sensuality. The sensuality of these images is important, for the Goddess is life-affirming and life-celebrating. It would be safe to say that almost all of these works were created by people whose senses were far more developed than ours generally are. Imagine the heightened sensuality associated with this art: What might be the colors, smells, tastes and sounds surrounding each image? What ceremonies and celebrations?

Each one of the images in this book is a treasure, a piece of sacred art. Thousands of devotees have stood before each of these works. Most are from cultures where what we call the spiritual is not separate from the everyday. This is not art as we know it, only to be looked at, studied or examined, and these images are not just abstract symbols. This is art that has been lived with, danced with, sung to, caressed, had earth and colors and fluids rubbed into it.

That so many of the ancient works have survived the centuries and millennia is a miracle. Think of how easy it is to break a piece of pottery or how awed we are by a piece of china that might have belonged to one of our grandmothers. Imagine how many more of these Goddesses there must have been, even in populations much smaller than today's. Consider that each of these images represents hundreds, perhaps thousands of other such figures which have been destroyed or are buried in museum vaults.

It is even more remarkable that these works and the reverence for the Goddess they embody have remained intact throughout generations of patriarchy. Only recently has the art of primal cultures—that is, of most of the world —been accepted into Euro-Western museums. These cultures, living closely to the Earth, generally honor the Sacred Feminine more than do industrialized societies. In North America, Native American peoples and cultures were destroyed so quickly and thoroughly that much of their art has been lost. In Africa, female power and pre-patriarchal African culture were eroded by the onslaughts of Christianity, Islam, colonialism and slavery.

Some of the more blatant examples of sexism occur in mislabeling images. Here I

Precolumbian priestess, Remojadas mislabeled "dancer in gaudy clothes." 200–500 c.e.

think of the many complex Great Goddesses, honored for millennia, now labeled simply "fertility figures." Or the figure, most likely a priestess dressed in a magnificent headdress and a short kilt, with bells on her ankles, a staff in one hand, a tambourine in another and a whistle in her mouth, who is described in a major text as "a dancer wearing gaudy clothes." Given that we are dependent on the personal and institutionalized biases of collectors, museums, scholars and publishers, the fact that female figures predominate in many old European, African and precolumbian American collections reflects the importance of women and the Goddess throughout human existence.

In the text, I have sought to bring alive the historical, anthropological, mythological, psychological and spiritual background of each piece. The historical and anthropological material serves to ground each image: It is important to realize that these works come from real people in real cultures who have lived and thrived on this planet. However, I have found that, in some cases, scholars disagree about some of the most basic facts. In the face of this, it has been important to me to be as factual as possible, while at the same time including my own intuitive understanding of each piece, which is based on long years of study and association.

THE GODDESS IS EVERYWHERE

In addition to showing powerful images, it was equally important to me to show the breadth of Goddess art. The number of similar images which reappear in cultures separated by thousands of miles as well as thousands of years is remarkable.

Most of the excellent current Goddess research has focused on Europe and the Near East. And yet all of us, no matter what our racial or spiritual heritage (for some of us, in an effort to find a sustainable spirituality, have adopted new paths), have spiritual and blood ancestors who revered the Goddess. She is an important part of the heritage of every person on the planet. In our search for roots and connection to the past, these images from our ancestors can impart stability and wisdom to us.

Research from every continent indicates that, from roughly 30,000 to 3000 b.c.e., women and the Goddess were honored. Most of these cultures were highly developed technologically and artistically, and some existed in peace for at least one thousand years. Women and men lived in partnership rather than domination.[1] Much of this art was made by peoples who honored women as the creators of life, primary providers of food, builders, artisans, healers, priestesses and leaders.

In most gathering and hunting cultures, women provide eighty percent (and the more stable portion) of the food supply. Many authorities now believe that women discovered agriculture and the healing power of herbs in their gathering activities. In Europe, it is likely that women also created many of the beautiful cave paintings, for the implements used for the paintings, as well as the hand imprints which appear on the cave walls, are the right size for the skeletons of the women and children of the time. Women, as the inventors of pottery, weaving and many other arts, are often the creators of the sacred art included here.

This passage from Heinrich Loth's *Woman In Ancient Africa* describes a representative example of the change in status that both the Goddess and women have undergone around the world:

When the transition from the original, primitive [sic] religions to belief in several gods took place the "Great Mother" lost her throne, but women as givers of life retained for a long time an important position of equal privilege which was supported by the collective consciousness of the peoples. . .even in places where matrilinearity had been replaced by patrilinearity the original matrilinear organization was still discernable in myths, religious beliefs, customs and traditions (*e.g.*, in the myths about Creation, sagas about the origins of the tribes, the Ultimate Mother, and even in the myths concerning kings.)

Although there are many valuable theories, no one knows why such a great shift occurred on our planet from peaceful, earth-loving cultures to those of the dominator, exploitative mode. Yet here we are, and we must change our course or we will destroy ourselves and the rest of earthly life with us. Throughout the past five thousand years of patriarchy, dedicated, visionary and brave souls have kept the Goddess, her traditions and her values alive. At this point in time, the Sacred Feminine in both women and men is the peacemaking impetus on the planet, the protector of life. The world is more ready for her than it has been for millennia and more in need of her than it has been for all of human existence.

This book represents peoples of the world who respect the Sacred Feminine, especially those who still honor the cycles of life and the planet. None of the cultures represented here is perfect and virtually all from 3000 b.c.e. to the present have overlays of patriarchy and its attendant ills: sexism, racism, colonialism, classism and homophobia. Yet all of these societies, as far as I have been able to determine —and here I am joined by many scholars— have their roots in matristic, Goddess-honoring cultures and retain some invaluable traditions.[2]

WHO IS THE GODDESS?

When I speak of the Goddess or the Sacred Feminine, I speak of a very simple yet complex concept. Ultimately, I see the Goddess as incorporating the full spectrum of existence, not just what we call "the feminine." The latter is actually a construct of a culture that divides existence into compartments, and in particular into the dualities with which we are so familiar: light/dark, female/male, mind/body, earth/spirit and so on.

The true nature of existence, including true human nature, I believe, is not so split. Acting and living from the integration of all these components is what I call spirituality. Thus, the Goddess represents a unity and wholeness which is the birthright and potential of every

human being. All of us, all of existence, are the Divine. In order to complete this whole by bringing back that which has been denied, I name the Divine the Goddess.

Paradoxically, we must use the limited language of our culture in order to free ourselves from its confines. Thus, the Goddesses included here often do represent what we call "the feminine," those parts of the whole which are missing in our dominant culture: nurturance, cooperation, compassion, sensuality, peacemaking and egalitarianism. What is different about the Goddess is that these qualities do not preclude others, such as power, fierceness or rationality—attributes which our dualistic worldview relegates to "the masculine" but which are also part of these Goddesses.

Sarvabuddha Dakini. Bronze. Nepal. c. 18th century c.e.

The Goddess also contains within her qualities which, along with the power of women, our patriarchal societies have denied and suppressed: emotions, particularly passionate ones, the body, and the earthly cycles of death and rebirth. These aspects of life have been attributed to the Dark Goddesses, and— along with the Earth, women and people of color—have been feared by the dominant Euro-Western culture. Yet the Dark Goddesses represent vital energies which we must reclaim if we are to live full and harmonious lives. When we honor these Goddesses, great benefits come to us, for they embody long-neglected riches.

Sometimes people ask me if these cultures have God images and myths as well. The answer is yes. While I feel strongly that life-affirming male images and myths are essential for our well-being, I have chosen to emphasize the Goddess because she and the values she represents have been so neglected in our culture, in both women and men. This choice is sometimes labeled "reverse sexism," and yet it really is a matter of just completing the picture. We are so unbalanced that my guess is we could all focus exclusively on the Goddess for the next few centuries, and maybe by then we would have come back into balance.

What does the Goddess represent to us at this point in time? She is love combined with power, creating the potential for a more powerful love and a more loving power. She is honesty and compassion. She is also joy and love of life, particularly life as we experience it through the Earth and her cycles. We live in a beautiful physical world, and in order to survive in it and fulfill our birthright of enjoying ourselves here, we must reclaim the Goddesses and myths which celebrate life and its cycles.

As I worked with the images I had collected for my classes, I saw that they fell into three categories: creation, including birth, nurturance, and the abundance of the natural world; transformation, meaning physical death and rebirth as well as the metaphorical deaths and rebirths of trance and descent to the underworld; and celebration, encompassing sexuality, sensuality and creativity. The unity of birth, growth, death and rebirth are the basis of the Goddess's teachings. We see them daily in the cycles of night and day, waking and sleeping, creating and letting go.

The Goddess is she who gives life and, when the form is no longer viable, transforms it through death. And then, through the exquisite pleasures of creativity and sexuality, she brings forth new life. All of us experience these cycles. They are what unite us in our human existence, and yet our ability to accept and work with them has been severely restricted in most patriarchal cultures, in which power means power-over, or coercion. In its place, we call for a power which expresses the innate life-force of co-creation.

MYTH AND POWER

Myths are transmitted by story, art and ritual. They provide us with a cosmology and a value system. They are also a form of condensed history, summarizing centuries of social, political and economic change in one story. Because they are alive, there are many versions of these stories, and they may vary from person to person. However, they are always important teaching devices which transmit the values of a culture, changing to meet the needs of the people.

Native American writer Jamake Highwater cites the Jungian philosopher Edward F. Edinger on the relationship between Western mythology and our survival: ". . . because Western culture no longer has viable, functioning myth, [it] therefore has no basis to affirm life." If one considers the traditional and popular mythology of Euro-Western culture, one can see that it is focused on unnatural destruction, including the denigration of women, who are the source of life.

Myths and rituals evolve from a particular time, place and people. They cannot be transposed from one culture to another. However, we can learn from one another's example. We must explore life-supporting world myths as well as create new ones, if we are to survive. In evoking a viable mythology for our times, it is important that we look to the past and to other cultures with respect, honor that which may be healing for our particular time and situation, and create new myths and deities to teach us how to ensure our physical and spiritual survival.

As I pointed out in my first book, *Womanspirit*, temporal power and spiritual power are inextricably intertwined. Spirituality is that state in which all of our actions and beliefs are integrated with one another, and this relationship recognized. The values we hold directly influence our behavior and how we structure our institutions. Time and again, myths associate women's loss of temporal power with their loss of sacred art and spiritual power.

In stories from the Kono of Guinea and the Kalabari of Nigeria, for example, women originally held the power through possession of ceremonial masks, which they lost to the men. It is the same in the Djanggawo creation myth of the Australian Aborigines, in which the two sisters are the most prominent figures until they leave their sacred objects unguarded and their brother and his companions steal them. Both the Africans known as Pygmies and peoples of the Amazon region in South America say that women used to own the sacred musical instruments, which were given to them by the deities. In each case, the men stole the instruments and thereby subjected the women; now women are threatened with death if they so much as look at these objects. By meditating on the art of the Goddess, singing her songs and saying her prayers, we can begin to reclaim her mythic power.

THE EARTH AS BODY OF THE GODDESS

I feel it is essential that we learn from one another's art and traditions if we are to live peacefully and prosperously together and cooperate in healing the planet's environmental crisis. In the process of doing this book, I have become aware on a far deeper level of how much we share with one another and with other forms of life on Earth. Yet we humans are now threatening not only our own existence, but that of the millions of other species on the planet.

In fact, at the current rate of destruction, which is attributable directly to human actions, approximately two hundred species *a day* become extinct. If we do not make drastic changes in our lifestyles, within the next decade we will lose such animals as the African elephant, and within fifty years, all of the Earth's remaining tropical rainforests will be gone. These figures are hard to believe and yet we must believe them, because they reflect the truth about the effects of patriarchal cultures on the planet.

Women have long been associated with—and controlled along with—the body and the rest of the natural world. Our desecration of the body of the Goddess is a direct result of our separation from Nature and the teachings of the Goddess that all of life is interrelated and sacred. One of the most popular environmental concepts is that of the Earth as a living organism, named Gaia after the Greek Earth Goddess. Many people are awakening to something primal peoples have always known, which is that we cannot drain Gaia's resources

Goddess with Sky Bar, perhaps representing the universal order. Chiapas, classic Maya, 7th century c.e.

without destroying ourselves and other forms of life.

Significantly, a key element in the Earth's survival, the Amazon rainforest, is named after the Mediterranean women warriors who were the last holdouts against the patriarchal Indo-European culture. Indeed, the tales of the Amazon River basin itself, as well as of other parts of the world, speak of tribes of strong women who lived independently from men. At this point, Gaia and the Amazon, and thus all life on our planet, are threatened. It is clear that in order to save ourselves—not to mention fulfill our true potential—we must honor Nature, the Goddess and women.

My hope is that this book will help us find ways to respect our diversity as we learn from and are enriched by all our traditions and symbols of the Sacred Feminine. Certainly the Goddess, who represents earthly life, unites us all.

LANGUAGE

As I have mentioned, we are faced with the problem of using the language of a patriarchal tradition which has destroyed or distorted all the cultures represented in this book. We must use this same language to describe the values and practices of these peoples and their Goddesses. The English language is quite rich in technical terms, yet poor in spiritual ones. Any translation can only be an approximation of the true meaning and power of the original language, especially when spoken in a ceremonial context as part of the life cycles of a whole culture. I have done my best to be respectful of each tradition, yet I recognize there is an inherent problem. My prayer is that this work will help heal the wounds.

The term "Goddess" is not used by all of the cultures represented here. Some of these images represent Ancestors, Spirits or other beings who are revered as greatly as Goddesses are in other cultures. I have chosen to use the word Goddess because it is the term which conveys the most power in the English language. By "Goddess" I mean the life force, both physical and non-physical; in other words, "all that is." As I have said earlier, I use a female word because we have suppressed the Sacred Feminine to such a degree that we have lost touch with the true full nature of existence.

I avoid the use of the terms "worship" or "Goddess-worshiping," as I feel they perpetuate the idea of a divinity who exists only outside ourselves. I have used the words "honor," "revere" and "respect" instead.

Because these Goddesses and their images and myths are alive as long as they are thought about, looked at and spoken of, I use the present tense in describing them. Instead of the exclusively Christian orientation of dating, I use the terms b.c.e. (before common era) and c.e. (common era) in place of b.c. and a.d.

I have written this book for both women and men. In the rare instances that I use the third person singular pronoun, I have chosen to say "she" and "her."

I am indebted to Jamake Highwater for the use of the term "primal" rather than "primitive," which has negative connotations inapplicable to the dignity and wealth of the cultures comprising most of human existence. It was Native American scholar Carol Lee Sanchez's writing which introduced me to the term "Euro-Western," which points out the ethnocentricity of the more commonly used term "Western." Many peoples of the Western Hemisphere are not primarily of European descent and have worldviews and practices which are very different from what is generally implied by the term "Western."

At times I speak of African, European, Native American, Oceanic, Arctic or Asian cultures or Goddesses. Of course, these are large areas and I try to be specific both geographically and culturally whenever my sources permit. From a worldwide perspective, sometimes important themes of a particular continent or broad region appear; focusing on this larger context is not meant to diminish in any way the rich variety of cultures within each area.

How To Use This Book

To me, and I hope to you, these images are alive and have much to teach us about living healthfully and in balance. For those who wish to bring the Goddess into their daily lives, I have included excerpts from traditional materials and created original prayers and meditations which are designed to evoke the qualities of a particular Goddess. It is important that we not just learn *about* the Goddesses, but that we invoke them and learn directly from them. These meditations and prayers are simply suggestions, and I urge you to adapt them to fit your own situation and needs. It will probably be easiest to read through a meditation before doing it. You might want to tape your favorites so that you can be more free to follow them.

With each image, imagine living in a culture in which these Goddesses are a part of everyday life. Picture them in public places or in your living room, or that you make offerings to them daily, as peoples have done throughout time.

One of art's most potent teachings can be gained by assuming the posture of a figure. I call this "somatic research." Often our minds, conditioned and indoctrinated as they have been, can prevent us from perceiving the truth; sometimes our bodies can tell us more.

I encourage you to take the pose of a Goddess in order to find out more about her and the qualities she conveys. If this is physically difficult for you, do as much as you can, or use your imagination instead. Try moving as she might move, speaking what she might say. This posture might be as simple as the hand gesture of Diana of Ephesus or as complex as the pose of Vajravarahi. Let yourself become her, and let her become you.

It is especially powerful to do the above exercise in front of a mirror, for seeing yourself in the pose of the Goddess usually adds a new dimension to your awareness of your body's potential. We are all part of the Divine, and the art in this book embodies this knowledge. As you begin to assume the poses of these images and notice how you feel, move,

act and speak from that place, you will remember parts of your true nature which have been lost. You will receive a direct transmission from the Sacred Feminine.

I suggest choosing one Goddess and working with her for a full week or season, spending time every day looking at her image, reading her story and/or doing a meditation on her. These creations have special meanings for each one of us and each of us will have a particular relationship to them. You will develop your own way of deepening your connection with these many aspects of the Sacred Feminine. You can work with different Goddesses at different times, or choose a sequence other than the one presented here. Your favorites will change as you change, depending on what energy is foremost in your life.

Here is a suggested program for a week's Goddess work. You could also choose to do this all in one session or as part of a group practice. I have used as an example my own work with the Great Goddess of Laussel, which I did at a time of great loss in my life.

Day 1: Contemplate the image and read the accompanying text.

Day 2: Set up a sacred place for this Goddess's image. Surround her with symbols of her qualities that are important to you. (For the Great Goddess of Laussel, I arrange around her image a moonstone for the lunar cycles and a pumpkin to represent the fullness of her harvest.)

Day 3: Do the meditation, take the pose of the Goddess and/or make up an affirmation for yourself that relates to her teachings for you. (I place my hands on my belly and spend ten minutes focusing on my center. I affirm that I will honor my cycles of rest and activity, emptiness and fullness.)

Day 4: Draw or mold this image. Let yourself be inspired by the Goddess so that you can create without judging your work.

Day 5: Imagine actually being in the presence of this sacred art. Interact with her through words and/or actions. (I imagine that I curl up in the Great Goddess of Laussel's lap.

I feel her abundance. She tells me that her waxing and waning are part of the cosmic flow and that it is fruitless to resist them. I find myself focusing on the abundance in my life and not just my loss.)

Day 6: Make up a prayer to her, asking that she come into your life. ("Great Goddess of Laussel, keeper of the mysteries, help me to learn how to be patient with the ebb and flow of life. Come to me to remind me of the turning of the cycles, that I will not despair in the hard times.")

Day 7: Create a ritual to activate this Goddess's energy in your life. (I walk through my house, stopping to acknowledge symbols of the different aspects of my life, remembering the richness of my life, naming my blessings and giving thanks.)

Certainly just looking at these images and allowing them to become part of your life will be extremely beneficial. Try taking this book out of doors and looking at them in natural sunlight. In any setting, these images will heal you, inspire you and impart to you their wisdom and saving grace. The more you work with them, the more the Goddess will grow in your life. To facilitate this process, I have listed those who have influenced my thinking as references for further study of each Goddess.

I have also listed organizations in the Resources section which you can contact to help protect the rights of indigenous peoples and support the survival of the Earth herself. Give to them in your prayers and in your actions—time, money and energy. For instance,

if you receive great inspiration from the Goddess Tara, send aid to Tibetan refugees and/or write letters to world leaders in support of human rights in Tibet. If you experience Spider Grandmother guiding you, work for Native Americans' rights to regain and keep their lands. We are privileged to share in the works of so many peoples from different parts of the world. The essence of the Goddess's teachings is that we are all interconnected. Please remember the cultures and the places that have given us these precious works.

LIVING WITH THE GODDESS

If you focus enough on the Goddess, it is almost as if she begins to notice you and takes you under her wing. She gradually begins to reveal herself in all her complexity, and sometimes in unexpected ways. This is an ongoing process, spiraling to deeper and deeper levels, always continuing.

As you spend time with these Goddesses and allow them to become part of your daily life, you will come more and more to embody the Sacred Feminine and complete your whole self. Let the Goddesses come into your meditations, your dreams, your work and the faces of people around you. You will begin to recognize and acknowledge the Goddess in your life and become fertile soil for her to grow in. Give her plenty of water, light and food and you will find yourself transformed by what grows inside you. You will have become the Goddess.

---

1 Examples of these long-lasting peaceful cultures are Old Europe, Minoan Crete, Catal Huyuk and the Cycladic culture.

2 For further background, see the bibliography. For a general overview, see Riane Eisler's The Chalice and the Blade, *Merlin Stone's* When God Was A Woman *and* Ancient Mirrors of Womanhood, *and Monica Sjöö and Barbara Mor's* The Great Cosmic Mother. *For Native America, Paula Gunn Allen's* The Sacred Hoop; *for Africa, Henri Loth's*

Woman in Ancient Africa; *for Hinduism, Ajit Mookerjee's* Kali: The Feminine Force; *for Buddhism, Tsultrim Allione's* Women of Wisdom; *for Europe, Marija Gimbutas's* Goddesses and Gods of Old Europe *and* The Language of the Goddess. *For practical ways of implementing some of these traditions in your daily life, see the exercises in my book,* Womanspirit: A Guide to Women's Wisdom.

Prajnaparamita, the Buddhist goddess whose teachings are the foundations of Mahayana Buddhism. Painting by Andy Weber.

The ancient Akkadians wrote that the Goddess known as Mami pinched off fourteen pieces of clay, and making seven of them into women and seven of them into men, She placed life upon the earth. The Dahomeans said that the Goddess known as Mawu built the mountains and the valleys, put the sun in the sky, and placed life upon the earth She had made. Chinese texts record that the Goddess known as Nu Kwa patched the earth and the heavens, when they had been shattered, and thus restored harmony and balance to the universe. In Mexico the Goddess known as Coatlicue lived high upon a mountain, in a misty cloud, and there She gave birth to the moon, the sun, and all other deities. Hesiod wrote that the Goddess known as Gaia gave birth to heaven, and mating with heaven, She brought forth the other deities. Sumerian texts tell us that the Goddess known as Nammu was called upon as the mother who gave birth to heaven and earth, and that She supervised the creation of all life by Her daughter Ninmah. In Egyptian hieroglyphics, it was written that the Goddess known as Au Sept was the oldest of the old, She from whom all becoming came forth. Indian records say that if the Goddess known as Devi were to close Her eyes even for a second, the entire universe would disapper.

—*The Birth Symbol* by Max Allen

PART ONE:

CREATION

CREATION

Ceramic vessel. Peru, c. 500–750 c.e.

Creativity—the power to manifest physical and psychic reality—is one of the Goddess's primary aspects. People have long identified the feminine as the source of all being. She appears as the Great Mother, the Sustainer of Life, the Cosmic Creatrix. It is from her that all life proceeds and to her that it returns. By its very nature, our ultimate cosmic origin comes before any gender or even species identity. But if one wishes to give human form to the Original Source, a female being, whether she be called Grandmother or Great Goddess, is the logical choice.

Archeologist Marija Gimbutas and art historian Max Allen, among others, assert that our oldest religious symbol represents the birth-giving power of the Great Goddess: It is a diamond-shaped figure with extending arms and legs; there is often an x-shaped fetus within the diamond. This abstraction first appeared in 25,000 b.c.e. and has since been encoded in the women's textiles of eastern Europe, Asia and the Pacific. Even today it is the most common motif in Eurasia and Indonesia. It is interesting to note that the diamond is the shape of the vulva at the crowning in birth, and the molecular shape of the female hormone.

The process of gestation and birth is one of the great mysteries of life. Our vastly complex bodies, personalities and characters seemingly emerge from microscopic specks. Surely, to our ancestors birth was the original mystery. They must have watched with awe the miracle of a child growing in and emerging from the body of a woman. Throughout the millennia, woman was revered for her unique abilities to give birth and sustain life, and because she was able to recreate both herself and her "opposite": a male child. As our forebears looked around at the rest of life, the trees, mountains and rivers, they must have thought that all this came from a very great woman's body—that of a Goddess, the "mother of all things."

The oldest recorded account of the creation of the universe, a Babylonian text, says that "When above the heavens had not been formed, when the earth beneath had no name,

Tiamat brought forth them both...Tiamat, the Mother of the Gods, Creator of All." The power of the Goddess's original act of creation could also be called upon during creation in the microcosm, as in a seventeenth century b.c.e. Babylonian text which encourages a woman in labor by telling the story of the Goddess Mami, who made the first person out of clay and blood. The female act of birth is sanctified even in St. Peter's Basilica in Rome, where the innermost shrine is enclosed by four pillars, three depicting the face of a woman in various stages of childbirth, the last the face of a newborn baby. Yoni-shaped leaves and "flowers" representing the female reproductive organs surround the mother.

Just as our ancestors honored woman's ability to create humans from her womb and feed them from her breast, they also honored the Earth as the Great Mother who nourishes us and from whose body we are all created. Rejoicing in her and celebrating the beauty of life were the natural expressions of our forebears' art and mythology. In time, as men and male deities took power, stories evolved which told of the Mother giving birth to or creating the Gods and Goddesses. Even in our patriarchal era, we can trace the original power of the Great Goddess in the art and myths of the Mothers of the Deities.

As weaver or dreamer or womb source of the universe, the Cosmic Birth Mother is the embodiment of creativity. At times this dynamic creativity has been associated with a particular life-giving element of Nature such as the sun. At others the nurturing motherliness of the Goddess is expressed through Mothers of the People, deities who protect, guide and provide a sense of common identity for the members of a culture. Perhaps it is because the Goddess spins life out of her own body that she remains so closely connected with her creatures. For she is also Lady of the Plants and Animals, moving easily between human and animal form, growing in the fields as grain—the One whose own body is the infinite variety of life forms she creates.

The Creation images I have chosen reflect the richness and abundance of earthly life. Each of these figures was lovingly made in awe and gratitude for all that the Goddess has given. In speaking of the Goddess's and human creative abilities, I mean the spiritual, psychic, healing and artistic powers, as well as those of physical birth and nurturing. Mothering is a powerful image for all acts of creativity, whether they be making a work of art, a relationship or a livelihood. By contemplating these images of the Creation Goddesses, we can learn more about the process of consciously giving birth and of consciously creating all aspects of our lives. As we honor the Creation Goddesses, we reclaim the source of existence. We rediscover life itself, as well as the possibility of living fully and creatively on the Earth.

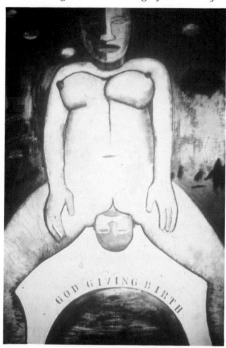

"God Giving Birth." Painting by Monica Sjöö.

THE GREAT GODDESS OF WILLENDORF

EUROPE, C. 25,000 B.C.E.

The mother of us all,
the oldest of all,
hard,
splendid as rock
whatever there is that is of the land
it is she
who nourishes it,
it is the Earth
that I sing.
—HOMERIC HYMN TO EARTH

We begin with the Great Goddess of Willendorf, Austria, for she is among the oldest artwork we have. Upper Paleolithic female figures such as this one made of limestone are found from the Pyrenees Mountains to Siberia, indicating that East and West were once united in honoring the Goddess. It appears that these images were an important part of daily life, for hundreds of them have been recovered, a considerable number given the size of the population at the time and the odds against any of them surviving through the millennia. Some of the statues were discovered in niches, their feet tapered for easier insertion in the ground, suggesting that they were part of an altar or shrine.

I call her the Great Goddess rather than her more traditional "Venus" label, for Venus is only one aspect of the all-encompassing Great Goddess, which this Lady surely represents. She is Earth herself, her body reflecting mountains and valleys, fields and rivers, her palpable sensuality a celebration of physical existence. Small and round, these Goddess figures fit easily into one's hand, a comforting reminder of our source in the Sacred Feminine.

The vast majority (over 90 percent) of human images from 30,000 to 5000 b.c.e. is female. Woman was recognized as the life-giver and sustainer, and she was most likely revered as a priestess for her ability to transcend her ego. American art historian Sandra Roos and Soviet archeologist Z.A. Abramova have independently concluded that Paleolithic peoples first honored woman in her human form, later developing the abstract idea of a Goddess.

In this statue, she contemplates the reality of her sacred physical presence. Rather than the features of personal identity, her ritual mask represents the waves of the primordial waters from which all life and consciousness arise. The Great Goddess of Willendorf is woman's faceless, egoless primal Self, peaceful in her body and her truly miraculous power—as woman and as Earth—to create life. Whether we, women and men alike, make art, children, community or cosmos, our act of creation derives from the same source: our Goddess-given power. We are re-enacting the Earth's capacity to create, and recreate, life.

O Great Mother, mother of us all, oldest of the old, come to me through the labyrinth of time to help me remember the wisdom of my forebears, the eternal life-giving power of woman.

CREATION

 *Imagine holding one of these Goddesses in your hand. Feel her roundness, the comforting security of it. Imagine carrying her throughout your day's work, on your travels, sleeping with her beside your bed, waking up beside her. What offerings would you make to the Mother of All?*

The Great Goddess of Laussel

The Great Goddess of Laussel, France, is the direct descendant of the Great Goddess of Willendorf. Carved in limestone over the entrance to a cave that was both a dwelling place and a ceremonial site, she was painted red, the color of life, blood and rebirth. With her left hand she points to her belly, and in her right she holds a horned crescent marked with thirteen lines, the number of moon cycles in a solar year.

The Great Goddess of Laussel represents an ancient honoring of the female body mysteries: the reflection in our bellies of the waxing and waning of the moon, the shedding of our menstrual blood as the moon sheds her brightness. She shows us how to touch our bodies lovingly, how to caress our bellies in appreciation of their magical powers of lunar renewal.

This Great Goddess embodies the wisdom of cyclic time: That all of existence evolves not in a straight line, nor even in a circle, but in a spiral of eternal growth. We come round to the same place on the wheel, yet we are at a different turn of the spiral. We have learned from the past, and are able to move through this new—and also old—place more easily than before.

Carved markings on other European Paleolithic artifacts, some shaped like the female body, correspond to the cycles of the moon. Perhaps these earliest human notations were women's records of their menstrual cycle, the precursors of writing and mathematics. The survival of gatherers, hunters and farmers depends on a knowledge of the moon's phases, and until recently lunar reckoning has been an integral part of all cultures.

People have used caves such as the one protected by the Great Goddess of Laussel throughout time as the most sacred sites for ritual rebirth. In many Paleolithic caves, formations shaped like breasts are painted red or black. The soot of countless fires has darkened the ceilings, and the floors have been beaten down by many feet. In some cases, one must crawl through long tunnels to reach the central chamber, at times with one's face to the ground. For most of us, this act would be an initiation in itself.

That this was only the beginning of Paleolithic ceremonies gives us a hint of the power of such experiences, and of the spiritual depth of the ancients. When we enter a cave or a cavelike space such as the Hopi *kivas*, we enter the womb of the Earth Mother, and our very molecules are rearranged by being inside her. Placing ourselves in her trust, we allow our old selves to fall away, and we emerge renewed.

O Great Goddess, teach me the sacredness of my body. Remind me how to touch my body lovingly, how to caress my belly in appreciation of its wisdom. Help me remember how to honor the female mysteries, the mysteries of blood and time.

Imagine such a Goddess carved over the entrances to our churches, synagogues, temples—or over the entrances to supermarkets and schools. Picture yourself making offerings to her when you enter a building. Remember that for 25,000 years almost all images of human beings were female, revered in public as sacred. How would living in such a culture make you feel differently about women? About the world?

THE CREATRIX

THE BIRD-HEADED SNAKE GODDESS

AFRICA, C. 4000 B.C.E.

*In the beginning, Eurynome, the Goddess of All Things, danced
upon the waves. From the wind stirred up behind her she made
the serpent Ophion. Ecstatically she danced, and Ophion curled
around her. Not long thereafter, she took the form of a dove and
laid the Universal Egg upon the waters. As she instructed,
Ophion curled seven times around the egg, until it hatched and
all the things of the world—the stars and planets, the mountains and rivers and all the living creatures—came pouring out.*
—PRECLASSICAL MEDITERRANEAN MYTH

The triumphantly female Bird-Headed Snake Goddess comes to us from pre-dynastic Egypt. Made of terra cotta, she emphasizes her breasts and buttocks with dignity and strength, reminding us of the power and beauty of the female body. The undulations of her form suggest those of a snake, and she simultaneously sends her energy deep into the earth and high into the sky. This statue is sometimes considered a worshiper of the Goddess, sometimes the Goddess herself. Yet she is both, reflecting the ancient knowledge that human and divine are one, just as she integrates the earthly snake and celestial bird. She is the Great Goddess, calling down blessings on her worldly self. Ultimately, she is a Goddess of Thanksgiving, celebrating life incarnate.

The bird and the Goddess have been associated for millennia, from the time of the Great Goddess of Willendorf to the Annunciation of Mary. Like the Goddess-Creatrix, birds are central figures in creation myths from all over the world. The Celtic Triple Goddess of Maiden, Mother and Crone is frequently depicted as a crane, while the symbol of the African Senofu tribe is the bird-woman Kono, their female ancestor. In the Hopi creation myth, a little wren assists two Goddesses in bringing life to Earth.

Bird, snake and Goddess have been with us since the beginning. Many of these myths also associate woman, bird and water, evoking the primordial birthplace in womb and ocean. Similarly, geometric markings on ancient Bird and Snake Goddesses represent life-giving moisture. As we remember, contemplate and dance the dance of the Bird-Headed Snake Goddess, we join earth and sky, human and animal, recognizing the divine as One in each and all of us.

*Take the pose of this Goddess, for she can teach you about the union of earth
and sky, spirit and body. Stand with your legs about a foot apart, knees slightly
bent. Feel your feet firmly planted on the ground, the muscles of your genitals and anus
relaxed. Thrust your buttocks out and your chest forward, making sure to keep breathing.
Raise your arms to the sky. And now imagine that you have a bird's head. Open your
mouth, and with your exhalation, let your breath become sound. It can be any sound
at all, but let it be your song. How do you feel with your body undulating, grounded
yet soaring? Continue to breathe fully, and sing the song of yourself as the Bird-Headed
Snake Goddess.*

9

THE CREATRIX

IXCHEL THE WEAVER

NORTH AMERICA,
8TH CENTURY C.E.

Old woman of all ages
Old woman of all ages
Holder of the memory
Starseed planted in your body
Life's web must be mended,
Spider Woman's crying
Each one of us is a weaver,
shining ones remembering
—CONTEMPORARY SONG
By Anne Williams,
Palenque, Mexico

Ixchel is the Mayan Goddess of the changing moon, weaving, prophecy, sexuality, healing and childbirth. She was revered throughout Southern Mexico, the Yucatan Peninsula and most of Central America, primarily from about 600 to 1500 c.e. She is still known as The Queen, Our Grandmother, Our Mother and The White Lady. For centuries, women have made pilgrimages to her holy places, including Isla Mujeres, the Island of Women.

In an early myth, Ixchel is the spider at the center of the world's web. Similarly, an Iroquois myth sees the lunar waxing and waning as the work of an old woman who sits in the moon, eternally creating and recreating a weaving. In Indonesia, a spinning spider represents the soul of the moon, and in Borneo the moon in the form of a spider creates the world. Yet Ixchel is also honored as a human woman, just as Navajo women weavers feel that they are directly inspired by Spider Woman's original act of manifestation.

In this terra cotta statue, Ixchel sits at her loom with her ever-present bird companion, the nest weaver, who is associated with the Goddess throughout the world. Ixchel sits easily and with great presence, for she is in the bliss of creativity, weaving the fabric of life itself. Each of us is a thread in her great pattern. Singing, spinning from her deepest being, she carefully smoothes the substance of every soul between her great fingers. She then chooses her color. Perhaps it is a clear red, or a peaceful blue, or a vibrant earth brown. Whatever color each of us is— whatever body, personality or character—we are purposefully created by the Goddess to make the Great Fabric of Life as it is meant to be.

Having chosen carefully, she takes a deep breath of eternity, exhales the life force into each being and begins to weave. And so your life, and all lives, begin. Sometimes choosing contrast, sometimes complementarity, picking the textures and colors which best suit one another, the Goddess weaves us together.

Feel the Goddess's selection in you, and her pattern in your life. Feel where you, and others, might have tried to interfere with the Great Weaver's design— where you tried to impose a "man-made" pattern onto Nature. Which is Ixchel's weaving? Which is yours? Where can a harmonious blend be made? Work to unravel the synthetic fibers from the fabric of your life and the life of the Earth. Help her to sort out the strands of the past and weave them into a new, brightly colored future.

THE CREATRIX

SPIDER THE CREATRIX

NORTH AMERICA, C. 1300 C.E.

In the beginning was thought, and her name was Woman...She is the Old Woman who tends the fires of life. She is the Old Woman Spider who weaves us together...She is the Eldest God, the one who Remembers and Re-members...
—*THE SACRED HOOP* BY PAULA GUNN ALLEN

Spider, an important being in many Native American mythologies, is represented in this shell gorget from Spiro burial mound in Oklahoma. The swastika in the center probably represents the four winds, directions and elements; the bands might be those of the snake, while the hands are a universal symbol of manifestation, blessing and healing.

A weaver like Ixchel, Spider is a symbol of the universe and of concrete manifestation. Primal cultures all over the world esteem spiders, who are protectors of sacred places. Myths and legends associate these tiny beings who miraculously weave their webs from their own bodies with the Creatrix and light, and with kind old women and weaving. Native American myths, including those from the Cherokee and Kiowa, honor Spider Grandmother as the only one of all the creatures who was able to bring back light from the land of the Sun People. She created our sun and gave us fire, an act immortalized in her web's sunraylike design.

Spider's web is also mirrored in the pattern of sound waves, and sound is one of her tools.

In author Merlin Stone's recounting of a North American Keres Pueblo myth, Spider Woman, Sussitanako, is in the great darkness of the Original Womb Void. She spins her web in the four directions and sings her two daughters into being. These children, Ut Set, mother of the Pueblo people, and Nau Ut Set, mother of all others, create the moon and sun from iridescent abalone shell, turquoise and brilliantly colored rocks.

With red, yellow, white and black clay, Spider Woman makes the people of the four races. Over each of us, as effortlessly and patiently as the spider spinning her web, she weaves a mantle of wisdom and love. She then attaches a strand of her web to the doorway at the tops of our heads—a psychic connection echoed by the !Kung of southern Africa, who say that their spirits fly to the sky along threads of spider silk when they are trance dancing. If we let this opening close and forget about our connections to Spider Woman, we lose our way. Yet we can keep this door open by chanting, and thus call on the universal wisdom of Spider Woman.

Sit in a comfortable position, your eyes closed, your spine straight but relaxed. As you breathe, create space between each of your vertebrae. Envision a strand of Spider Woman's web attached to the top of your head. Feel your spine lengthening with this contact with the Creatrix. Now feel the muscles of your scalp relaxing, your brain relaxing. Feel her being touching yours, her thoughts and messages traveling easily along her web to you. Ask her what you can do, in a concrete way, to help reweave the web of life. Listen carefully to her answers. When you are finished, give thanks to Spider Woman, honoring your connection to her. Slowly open your eyes, retaining the thoughts she has for you.

THE CREATRIX

One day, Mother Woyengi stepped down to earth in a lightning-flash. She began shaping the earth into people, lifting each one to her nostrils and giving it the breath of life. She whispered in their ears, "You can choose to be a man or woman. You can also choose the life you want." And so the new wisewomen, farmers, potters, musicians, fishers, weavers, hunters and mothers-of-families-to-be felt power and character stream into them. Woyengi then took them to two streams and said, "The stream on this side leads to luxury; the stream on that side leads to ordinariness. You've chosen the kind of life you want." When the people who had asked for riches, fame or power stepped into their stream, they found it fast-flowing and dangerous with weeds and currents. The people who had asked for humble, helpful or creative lives stepped into the other stream and found it shallow, clean and clear. So, one after another, Woyengi's children began floating or swimming in the stream of riches and the stream of ordinariness, and the waters carried them away to irrigate the world with the human race.

—STORY OF THE NIGERIAN IJO PEOPLE

*A*kua'maa (singular: *Akua'ba*) are beautiful wooden lunar figures that the Asante women of Ghana traditionally use to ensure the continuity of their matriliny, or descent through the female line. Akua'ba literally means "Akua's child," from the story of a woman named Akua who, by carrying one of these figures, became pregnant and gave birth to a healthy, beautiful daughter. These sculptures are washed, dressed, adorned with jewelry, nursed and carried on the backs of women as an act of magic—that is, an act of encouraging change through thoughts and symbolic actions.

These images resemble the shape of the *ankh*, the ancient Egyptian symbol for life, which is related to our contemporary symbol for woman. All of life depends on the female and her moon cycle, reflected in the peaceful lunar face of the Akua'ba. Like the *Kachina* dolls of the North American Hopi, these figures are used to instruct the children in traditional ways. They are dolls in the original sense of the word, deriving from the same root as "idol": a piece of sacred art.

Mawu is the creatrix of life and mother of the deities for the inhabitants of the People's Republic of Benin (formerly Dahomey). In their thealogy, we each contain a part of Mawu called the *Sekpoli*, which is similar to the Euro-Western concept of the soul. Because we are all part of Mawu, fighting and aggression are self-destructive.

May the moon-faced Akua'ba inspire me to pray for daughters who are healthy, both physically and spiritually, that the motherline may continue. May I know that to love life, I must love the female.

15

BIRTH

ALL MOTHER AND THE DJANGGAWO SISTERS
AUSTRALIA, 20TH CENTURY C.E.

She made us talk like people; she gave us understanding. She made our feet, cut fingers for us, made our eyes for seeing, made our heads, made anger and peace for us, made our belly and intestines, gave us energy to move about—made us people.

—A GUNWINNGU WOMAN

The Australian Aborigines are the oldest continuous culture on Earth. This rock painting (top) from Arnhem Land in Northern Australia depicts Old Woman or All Mother. She gives birth to the Ancestors in the Dreamtime, a dimension which is the source of, and occurs simultaneously with, what we ordinarily perceive as reality. All Mother's children stand beneath her in ceremony. Her large vulva reflects her cosmic creativity, while her featureless face, like that of the Great Goddess of Willendorf, reminds us of her transpersonal nature. Some say that she first emerged from the underworld as her alter ego, Ngalijod, the Rainbow Serpent, and gave birth to the First People. After they were born, she brought them to life by licking them.

The artist Mawalan, assisted by Wangjuk and others, created a bark painting (bottom) of the life cycle of the Djanggawo Sisters, who in some stories are the daughters of All Mother. The Sisters came from Bralgu, the Land of Eternal Beings, and are at Arnhem Bay, where they are forever giving birth to the first Aborigines. This event is annually recreated in Aboriginal ceremony to this day. Their children, as well as their menstrual and birth blood, are contained in the circles surrounding them.

The Djanggawo Sisters are magical beings who fashioned parts of the land, the waterholes and trees. Even rituals were born from them, and pieces of their long clitorises became the first sacred objects. The Tiwi Aborigines say that when the two daughters of Mother of All became old, they flew into the sky with their torches—one gold, one silver. The gold torch became the Sun; the silver became the Moon.

They are sacred, those young girls of the western tribes, with their menstrual flow...
Sacred, with flowing blood—young girls of the western clans...
They are always there, sitting within their huts like sea-eagle nests, with blood flowing...
Flowing down from the sacred uterus of the young girl...
Sacred young girls from the western tribes, clans from the Woolen River:
Blood, flowing like water...

—POEM FROM GOULBURN ISLAND,
OFF ARNHEM LAND

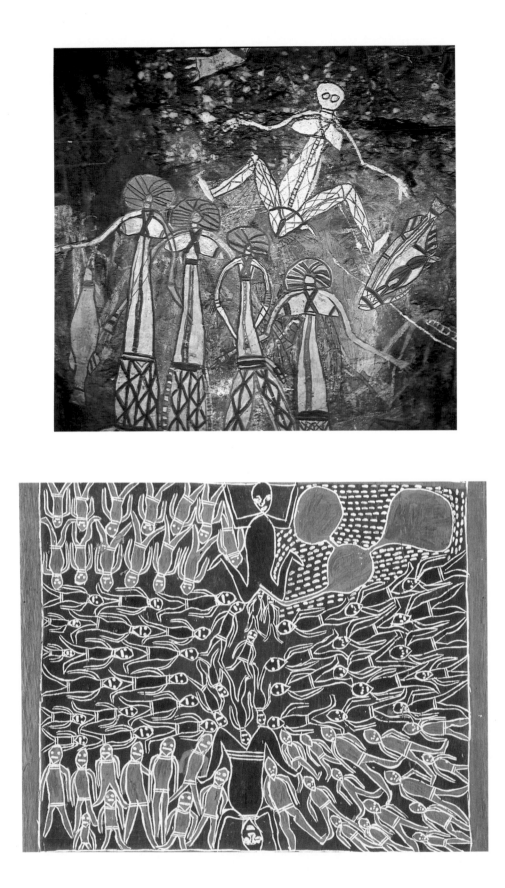

17

BIRTH

TLAZOLTEOTL

NORTH AMERICA, 15TH CENTURY C.E.

In the house with the tortoise chair
she will give birth to the pearl
to the beautiful feather
in the house of the goddess who sits on a tortoise
she will give birth to the necklace of pearls
to the beautiful feathers we are
there she sits on the tortoise
swelling to give us birth
on your way on your way
child be on your way to me here
you whom I made new
come here child   come be pearl
be beautiful feather

—AZTEC POEM TO EASE BIRTH

Just as the Goddess Ixchel weaves our destinies from the fabric of existence, so also woman weaves living beings from the tissues of her body. And just as Spider spirals out from the center of her web, and just as life itself evolved from the single-celled amoeba, so also woman, in the ultimate act of creation, builds a living being around her fertilized egg.

In this ceremonial statue made of aplite speckled with garnets, the Goddess Tlazolteotl portrays the heroic aspect of birthing. She is the image of woman reclaiming her power through the act of consciously giving birth. The purpose of ceremony and ritual is to bring full consciousness to all our actions, and it is possible to experience trance, or bliss, even in the most challenging moments of life.

The Aztecs accorded special respect to a woman who died in childbirth and honored her as a warrior. Some of the most demanding Native American and Samoan rituals are said to inspire men to the courage of a birthing woman. Men's and children's participation is an important part of conscious birthing, and of learning to live fully and peacefully. Once one knows the cost as well as the miracle of creation, one values life much more.

Author Vicki Noble says that in childbirth a woman is

> quintessentially shamanic. A woman about to give birth stands at the gateway between death and life. She peers into the death realm, not knowing for certain if she will come out alive, and she reaches over there to bring through another new soul. To face death without fear to save a soul, is the feat that all apprentices must master before they can call themselves shamans. Most forms of what we call shamanism are takeoffs on the original prototype, a mother giving birth.

Tlazolteotl, help me reclaim the power of consciously giving birth in all aspects of life. Goddess of the Earth, show me how to be strong in the face of fear, focused in the face of pain, knowing that to create new life, I must at times offer my life.

19

BIRTH

The Birth Goddess of Catal Huyuk
Asia Minor, 7th Millennium B.C.E.

This baked clay statue shows the Goddess giving birth on a lion throne. She was found in a grain bin, indicating her association with fertility, at Catal Huyuk in what is now Turkey. The largest and richest Neolithic site of the Near East, Catal Huyuk was a town covering thirty-two acres, with flourishing trade, agriculture and crafts. It was inhabited from approximately 6500 to 5600 b.c.e., a period of uninterrupted peace and prosperity. The Goddess was pre-eminent, appearing as a young girl, a mother and an old woman. Women were the center of life, yet the social structure was egalitarian.

At Catal Huyuk is a birthing shrine with red-painted floors and images of the ubiquitous Open-legged Goddess in labor. Most likely, women went there to give birth in a cere-monial context, surrounded by music, priestesses and midwives. The people of Catal Huyuk venerated death in a similar manner. They buried their dead, some painted with red ocher, the iron-rich earth used to symbolize rebirth, under the elevated platforms on which they sat, worked and slept. As an indication of their status, the women were buried under the larger, centrally located platforms.

The art of Catal Huyuk reflects the indi-visibility of the Birth Mother and the Death Mother. They are both guardians of the gate-way to earthly existence; one does not exist without the other. On the wall of a funeral shrine, vulture beaks take the place of nipples in sculpted breasts, and frescoes portray priestesses as Vulture Goddesses picking clean the bones of the dead.

Many cultures have held vultures in high regard. In Egyptian hieroglyphs and Hebrew documents, the notation for "vulture" is the same as that for "compassion" and "womb" or "mother." Some Native Americans call vultures "peace eagles" since they do not kill to eat, and the birds are sacred to the divine Tibetan Dakinis for their assistance in the death-rebirth process.

There is a possible correlation between the reverence for birth and death by the people of Catal Huyuk and their centuries of peace and abundance. In some North American tribes, women decided whether or not to go to war, for they were the ones who gave life. In a similar way, the people of Catal Huyuk, who ritually honored birth, would have been less eager to engage in conflicts. Accepting death as a natural part of the cycle, they would not have needed to project fear of death onto supposed "enemies" as we do, much less stockpile far more weapons than they could ever use. Rather than drain their resources, they acknowledged the cycles of life and made the best use of their bounty. Like the Minoans, Hopi and other matristic cultures, they could focus their energies on creating a harmonious life, rather than on supporting conflict and squandering reserves on unnecessary "defense."

Imagine life in such an egalitarian society, one where women were honored. . .Think of birth as a major sacred event. . .What would it be like to live over the bones of generations upon generations of your ancestors?. . .Imagine living in a culture that was peaceful for a thousand years, having a heritage without war, draft or military taxes. Consider centuries of human existence spent creating art, performing ceremony, growing or gathering food and living in harmony with other forms of life. . .What would it be like if your society's resources were focused on sustaining and rejoicing in life? What might your daily life be like in such a culture? How would you feel about yourself and the world?

CREATION

BIRTH

GWANDUSU

AFRICA, C. 14TH–15TH CENTURIES C.E.

Woman is like God,
because she gives birth to the people.
—AFRICAN PROVERB

In Africa, to which much evidence points as the birthplace of the human race, artistic images of mother and child are widespread. Unlike many depictions of Euro-Western Madonnas, however, the emphasis is on the mother rather than the child. Traditional African societies consider children divine gifts and value women as the mothers of culture, as well as for their equally miraculous ability to conceive, birth and feed their physical children. The Mande of West Africa, for instance, believe that one derives one's character, capabilities and destiny from one's mother.

This wooden statue, of a style known as *Gwandusu*, was made by the Bamana people of Mali. Such sculptures are enshrined as part of the Gwan, an association of women who desire children. Once a year the statues are washed, oiled, dressed and decorated with beads. The power of this figure is indicated by her seated position and headdress. She might be a chieftain, the founder of a lineage or clan, or the Primordial Mother described in many African legends.

Kate Ezra explains, "Gwandusu's name implies a character that embodies extraordinary strength, ardent courage, intense passion and conviction, and the ability to accomplish great deeds." The people describe the statues themselves as "extraordinary and marvellous things. . .that could be looked at without limit."

Gwandusu's pose is reminiscent of Egyptian statues of the Goddess Isis nursing Horus or holding Pharaoh on her lap, and of the Sumerian description of the Goddess Inanna with her consort Dumuzi. The Egyptian hieroglyph for Isis also signifies "throne," supporting some scholars' belief that African sculptures of women holding chiefs' stools reflect the power of women as the source of all life and culture.

Speak the names of the Original Mothers:

The Senufo of the Ivory Coast call her Maleeoo, Ancient Mother, the creatrix of culture itself, who teaches her daughters how to maintain harmony among the people;

The Ibo of Nigeria call her Ala, ruler of all living and dead, giver of children and crops, and build houses for her and her companions;

The Bamana of Mali call her Moussou Koroni Koundye, the Old Woman with White Hair who created plants, people and animals, she who dissolved her form to become air, wind and fire.

CREATION

BIRTH

Precolumbian bowls with a three-breasted base such as this ceramic one are similar to vessels from Peru, Bronze Age Poland and ancient China. The Greeks said that the first bowl was modeled after the breast of Aphrodite. For, of course, if we are raised naturally, mother's breast is the first "bowl" from which we feed.

Breasts have always been a symbol of physical and spiritual nourishment. In Africa, some older Yoruba women retain the custom of holding their breasts as greeting to someone they are especially happy to see. This gesture of the abundance and generosity of the female is repeated in art around the world. In European Paleolithic caves, breastlike stalactites were painted with red ocher, the color of life. According to the Diné (Navajo), the Goddess Estanatlehi shook colored flour from her breasts and made it into present-day people. The word "galaxy" comes from the ancient Greek *laktos*, meaning "milk," and myth has it that the Milky Way is the outpouring of the Goddess's breasts.

Mountains throughout the world are also associated with the Goddess and her breasts. Mt. Sinai is known as the Mountain of the Moon, and the Native American Ohlones saw Twin Peaks in San Francisco as the Goddess's breasts. Chomolungma (Mt. Everest) is so sacred as the Mother Goddess of the Snows to Himalayan peoples that it was considered a sacrilege to climb on her, much less "conquer the mountain" as Euro-Westerners do.

When we objectify woman and her body, and when women are denied the right to choose breastfeeding, we fall out of harmony with our true nature and suffer a continual state of scarcity. When we honor the Sacred Feminine and the Goddess, we are fed. Source of life-sustaining food and warmth, identified with the comforting sound of the heartbeat, the breast is reassurance of the abundance of the Earth Mother and of life itself.

Imagine holding this bowl. It is filled with the milk of the Great Mother. Feel the curves of the breasts with your fingers. Touch the nipples. Feel the roundness and the substance of this sacred bowl, the fluidity of the liquid. Raise the bowl to your lips and drink the Goddess's milk. Know that you are well fed, physically and spiritually. Remember that you are the child of the Goddess.

NURTURANCE

DIANA OF EPHESUS

ASIA MINOR, 2ND CENTURY C.E.

There are numerous statues of the many-breasted Diana of Ephesus, embodiment of the abundance of the Goddess. This one is made of alabaster and bronze. Nourishing all life, Diana has many breasts because she has many children to feed. Her hands form the gesture of bestowing worldly and spiritual blessings. Surrounded by the animals she sustains, she is crowned with the Goddess's sacred vessel, and the lunar disc makes a halo around her head. Like the Great Goddess of Willendorf, Diana is the Earth herself, whose mountains are breasts and whose body is a dwelling place for all living creatures. Dark like the Earth, she is the forerunner of the Dark Madonna of later times.

The Diana of the classical period is a relatively recent epiphany of the Goddess known since prehistoric times as the Queen of Heaven. Even in the patriarchal era, her worship was so strong that her temple at Ephesus on the coast of Asia Minor was the largest temple of classical times and was considered one of the Seven Wonders of the Ancient World. Made of marble and gold and overflowing with treasures, including this statue, it attracted more pilgrims than any other temple in the ancient world. In his letter to the Ephesians, St. Paul decries the city's outspoken women, and story has it that his missionary speech there was drowned out by chants of "Di-ana, Di-ana, Di-ana!"

Legend says that the Virgin Mary retired to this Goddess site, died there and ascended to heaven. Appropriately, in 451 c.e. the Council of Ephesus proclaimed Mary "Mother of God," thus officially supporting her worship in the Christian Church. The Council rededicated Diana's temple as a shrine to Mary, who became the next link in an unbroken chain of Holy Mothers stretching back to the beginnings of human history.

Great Mother, let me remember the abundance of your Being. Feed me with your many breasts. Remind me that, when I live by your ways, there is plenty for all your children.

27

NURTURANCE

THE WOODLANDS NURSING MOTHER

NORTH AMERICA,
13TH—14TH CENTURIES C.E.

some make potteries
some weave and spin
remember
the Woman/celebrate
webs and making
out of own flesh
earth
bowl and urn
to hold water
and ground corn
—"WOMANWORK" BY PAULA GUNN ALLEN

The Woodlands Nursing Mother, which is actually a ceramic pot, exemplifies the ancient and worldwide association of vessels with women, creation, nurturance and spiritual power. The womb is the alchemical container of life, as is the breast for food. Echoing the Goddess's creation of people from clay, in many cultures women have traditionally been the potters. Speaking of the origins of human culture, Buffie Johnson says, "On an archaic level, all pottery was created by women. The vessel is woman. Clay became sacred to the female; no man could be present at the making of a pot, nor could he touch the taboo clay until the invention of the potter's wheel."

In later times, this relationship has linked the Feminine with spiritually symbolic containers: African divination bowls, the European alchemical vessel, the witch's cauldron of healing herbs, the Arthurian Holy Grail, and the Christian chalice and baptismal font.

This lovely sculpture from present-day Illinois was made by the prehistoric Woodlands Indian culture known as the Mound Builders. The Woodlands people live in the midwestern, middle and southern United States; their art is filled with snake and spider motifs, such as our carving of Spider. The Mound Builders are perhaps best known for the Serpent Mound in Ohio, the beautiful, undulating, quarter-mile-long earth sculpture of a snake with an egg in its mouth. A traditional Asian symbol for lunar eclipse, the snake-and-egg motif appears in many Goddess creation myths, as in the story of Eurynome which appears with the Bird-Headed Snake Goddess.

In this Mother's pose we can see qualities of Woodlands Indian life: respecting the cycles of Nature and living lightly on the land, with awareness of the Spirits who inhabit the woods. Her pose is simultaneously relaxed and regal, a combination rarely seen in Euro-Western culture. She serenely nurses her child, an experience that many women describe as extremely sensual and erotic. The ceremonial regard for the birth process is beautifully expressed in this Diné (Navajo) prayer:

. . .With long life-happiness surrounding me may I in
blessing give birth! May I quickly give birth!
In blessing may I arise again, in blessing may I
recover,
as one who is long life-happiness may I live on!
Before me may it be blessed, behind me. . ., below me
. . .above me. . ., in all my surroundings may it
be blessed, may my speech be blessed! It has
become blessed again, it has become blessed again,
it has become blessed again, it has become blessed
again!

—A DINÉ RITUAL FOR GIVING BIRTH

CREATION

NURTURANCE

AMATERASU

*The radiance of the Sun Goddess filled the universe,
and all the deities rejoiced.*
—*RECORDS OF JAPAN*, 8TH CENTURY C.E.

There are Sun and Fire Goddesses throughout the world. In fact, in most primal cultures the sun is female. For the Cherokee the Sun Goddess is Igaehindvo, and the Celtic Fire Goddess Brigit became the Irish Christian St. Bridget. Merlin Stone tells us of Sun Woman of the Australian Arunta, Akewa of the Toba of Argentina, Sun Sister of the Arctic Inuit, and Allat of the Arabs. The Sun Goddess of ancient Anatolia controlled the right of rulership, just as the Japanese imperial family traces its lineage directly to the Goddess Amaterasu.

Amaterasu Omikami, the Great-Goddess-Spirit-Shining-in-Heaven, Creatrix Goddess of the sun, weaving and agriculture, is the most ancient Japanese deity. To this day, she is honored at public and private Shinto shrines throughout the country. Many elderly Japanese retain the custom of bowing and making offerings to her each morning as she rises.

In this detail from a colored woodcut by Utagawa Kunisada, Amaterasu appears in all her glory to the other deities. In the myth which leads up to this moment, her brother Susanoo has disrupted the natural and social orders of heaven through physical violence, particularly violence against women. Eventually one of the Goddess's weaving women dies of a wound to her vulva. Amaterasu is so enraged that she closes herself into a cave and refuses to come out. As in the Greek myth of Demeter and Persephone, without the Goddess all life begins to wither and die.

The other Goddesses and Gods try to lure Amaterasu out. Since celebration is an integral part of worship, they decide to have a party. Eight hundred of the deities gather in front of the cave, and their music and song can be heard throughout the world. Knowing that Amaterasu has never seen herself, they set up a mirror opposite the cave's entrance. At the high point of their revelries, the Goddess Ame no Uzume, sometimes represented as elderly, performs a particularly erotic dance. The spectators become so vocal in their appreciation that Amaterasu is overcome by curiosity. She emerges from her cave and for the first time sees her own radiance and glory. Enticed by the erotic sacred play of the Crone, the Sun Goddess returns, and life is renewed.

Just as it was in the myth, the world is now in danger of dying. To restore the natural and social order necessary to survival, it is essential that patriarchal violence cease. We must also reveal the brilliance of our inner light, which we have hidden for too long. Let us reclaim the mirror in its original sense, "to marvel at," so that we may each recognize our own radiance, come out of our caves and shine our light onto the world.

Amaterasu, give me your mirror, that I may daily see my own reflection in your face.

FIRE AND SUN

MAHUIKA

Fire was almost lost to the world. But as the flood waters rose about me I sent the last seeds of fire into the earthly trees—the kaikomako, mahoe, totara, patete and pukatea—and asked these trees to be the guardians of fire forever.

—"MAHUIKA" BY PATRICIA GRACE

Long ago, Mahuika, also known as Mahuea, brought the Maori people to New Zealand, where she also discovered the art of making fire. In this beautiful oil painting by Robyn Kahukiwa, Mahuika presides over her creation, the flame of life and transformation. She holds one of her fiery children, who are represented by her flaming fingernails. The trickster God Maui once tried to take her power by drowning these offspring in a stream, which is illustrated on the left of this painting. But Mahuika kept fire safe for her people by placing the remaining flames in the sacred trees. She then taught human beings how to make fire for themselves by rubbing her digging stick in a piece of grooved wood, as shown on the right.

Myths around the world describe the Goddess as the keeper of the flame, for woman is the custodian of the hearth and spiritual power. The Egyptian Nut and the Aztec Tlazolteotl both give birth to the sun, while numerous legends say that women keep fire in their genitals. Throughout most of human history, and in many parts of the world today, people have a daily and direct relationship with fire in its elemental form. Although this primal experience has largely been lost in technological cultures, we still depend on fire for survival.

Fire is also a worldwide metaphor for spiritual awakening. The story of Mahuika echoes the timeless Hindu tradition of *shaktipat*, whereby transmission from teacher to student occurs in the form of a flame taken from a central fire. This image of Mahuika captures the original transmission of the flame of life itself through the Sacred Feminine.

FIRE AND SUN

NUT

The Adorer.
Receiving Arm.
Arm of Light.
Brilliant One.
The One of the Rays.
Arm of Dawn.
　　　—*THE SHRINES OF TUT-ANKH-AMON*
　　　　By Alexandre Piankoff

Nut is an ancient African Goddess of the Cosmos, surviving from before the enforced unification of Egypt's Upper and Lower Kingdoms in about 3000 b.c.e. by the people of the God Horus. In this painting from the Temple of Hathor, Nut arches protectively yet gracefully over the Earth. From the horned crescent at her feet grows the Tree of Life, venerated throughout the ages. Rooted in the soil and spreading its branches against the sky, the tree unites her earthly and celestial aspects. On Nut's horizon sits Hathor, cow-headed Goddess of music, dance and love.

Each morning Nut gives birth to the sun, which radiates from her womb. Each evening she swallows it up and it travels through her night-sky body, which "causes the stars to manifest their souls." The next day at dawn, the sky turns rose-colored from her birth blood, as the Goddess again brings forth the sun in a continuous cycle of darkness and light.

As genetrix of the sun, Nut is the Mother of Life. From her breast flows the cosmic rain-milk which nourishes the life she creates and protects so beautifully. The hieroglyph for her name is thought to represent both "womb" and "waterpot" and her body is covered with the worldwide Goddess symbols for water, dew, snake and fecundity. Nut teaches us that darkness is necessary for light, that consuming life gives life and that death brings rebirth. Out of the vast darkness of the void, which is her womb, all existence arises.

When you go walking, imagine that the Goddess Nut arches above, protecting you. Feel her presence all around you. Know that her nurturing milk, the food of the universe, is available to you whenever you need it. At sunset, think of her swallowing up the sun. Offer up your day to her, to be transmuted within her great being. At dawn, imagine the sun emerging from her womb, and with it you, reborn.

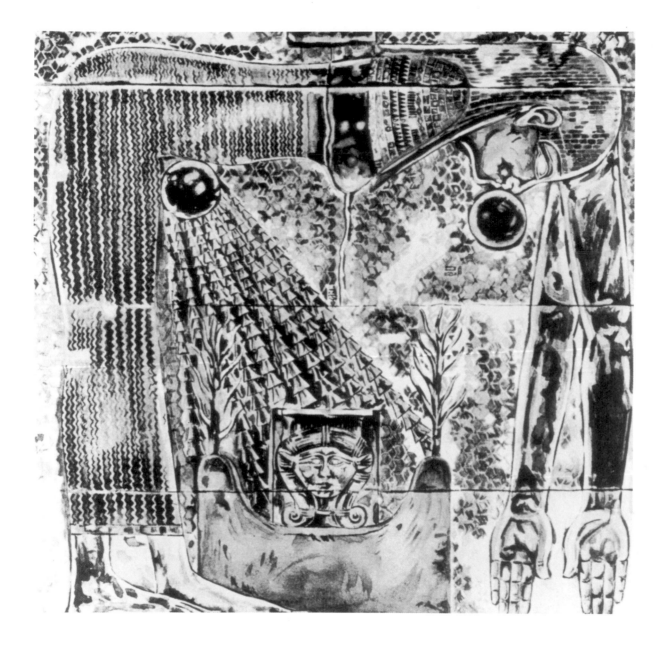

F I R E   A N D   S U N

QUEEN MAYA

ASIA, 2ND CENTURY C.E.

When Queen Maya conceived the Buddha, the ten thousand worlds quaked. A boundless light spread through them, healing the sick and freeing those in prison. Even the fires went out in all the hells. A refreshing breeze began to blow, and musical instruments played by themselves. Water burst from the earth and flowed in cooling streams to the ocean, which became sweet. Lotuses of the five colors bloomed on the land, and it rained flowers from the heavens. Queen Maya could feel the quickening embryo like a white thread passing through a transparent jewel in her womb.

—*JATAKA* STORY

Queen Maya, mother of the historical Buddha, is depicted in many beautiful works of art which, as Joseph Campbell says, illustrate the female origins of Buddhism. This is true in the literal sense, for Queen Maya was the mother of Prince Siddhartha, who became the Buddha. It is also true metaphysically: The Goddess Prajnaparamita, whose name means "highest perfect wisdom," is called the spiritual mother of all the Buddhas—that is, the source of enlightenment itself.

In this five foot high marble plaque, the top right carving shows Queen Maya dreaming of the conception of the Buddha; on the top left, she meets with her counselors to interpret the dream. On the bottom right, she is in the sacred Goddess grove of Lumbini, where she has stopped to worship. There, supported by a tree—and by implication the sacred forces of the natural world of her creation—she gives birth to the Buddha. On the bottom left she presents her baby to a tree divinity.

The power and eroticism of Queen Maya's poses are striking. In the birth scene, her body mirrors the sensuality and life force of the tree. Maya is often painted or carved in the same pose as the strong and graceful Hindu Tree Goddesses. Classical Indian literature describes women who, in a union of divinity with fertility, bring a tree to fruition with a kick (see insert). Maya too is pictured with her foot resting on the tree.

Trees are the largest and oldest living beings on the planet, and for many reasons we depend upon them for our survival. In an attempt to prevent deforestation of their land, members of the woman-led Chipko movement in India chain themselves to trees. There is an integral relationship between maintaining spiritual practices which honor Nature and our ability to preserve the planet. As well as providing oxygen, trees connect Earth and sky and have long been regarded as sources of wisdom, protection and nurturance. Asherah was the Near Eastern mother of the deities; the Hebrew word *asherah* is translated as "grove." Groves were also sacred to Artemis/Diana, and the Minoan and Mycenean Great Goddess is often represented as a tree or pillar. Even today, in Great Britain, Greece, Japan and India, trees are hung with prayers to the Goddess.

You can draw on the resources of the Earth by imagining yourself as a great tree. If possible, do this meditation actually leaning against a tree. Imagine roots extending down from the base of your spine, or, if you are standing, from your feet. Think of these roots as spreading wide, reaching deep into the layers of the Earth. Let your roots travel down past the roots of other plants, past worms and creatures of the soil, down past the layers of rock and crystal. Feel yourself drawing up, through your root system and into your body, all the energy you need from Mother Earth. Allow yourself to be nourished and fed by her. . . And now, visualize the forests of the Earth protected and flourishing. Bring your awareness back up along your root system and into your body. In a prayer, thank the trees closest to you.

MOTHERS OF THE DEITIES

Hahai'i Wuhti

"In the summertime we will come again," [the kachinas] sang. "We will come as clouds from the west, the south, the east, and the north to bless the Hopi people and to water their fields and crops. Then the Hopis will see their corn plants majestically growing. They will be so happy they will joyfully sing praises to the spiritual beings who brought moisture. At the edge of the cornfield a bird will sing with them in the oneness of their happiness. So they will sing together in tune with the universal power, in harmony with the one Creator of all things. And the bird song, and the people's song, and the song of life will become one."

—*THE BOOK OF THE HOPI* BY FRANK WATERS

Hahai'i Wuhti (or Hahay' wuuti) is the Mother of the Hopi Kachinas. The Hopi, whose name literally means "people of peace," remain some of the most balanced, strong and peaceful people in the world. They are matrilineal, the stewardship of the land (for the Hopi knew that no one can *own* the Earth) passing from mother to daughter.

Kachinas are the Supernaturals—who, according to Frederick Dockstader, are the female ancestors—as well as the Spirits of animals, plants and other aspects of Nature. They link human with divine, maintain order in the community and bring rain to the sandy soil. The Hopi believe that survival would be impossible without the Kachinas. In fact, they say that they were led to their harsh, beautiful mesas so that they would, of necessity, maintain their rich and powerful ceremonies.

The Hopi give their children Kachina dolls to teach them the various qualities and aspects of the supernatural beings. At birth, each child is given a two-dimensional carving of Hahai'i Wuhti and a perfect ear of corn. The Kachina dolls are not toys, but everyday sacred objects. Full-dimensional dolls such as this one of Hahai'i Wuhti are made for grown girls, and more recently these dolls have become an art form. Kachinas are also represented in beautiful, elaborate dance costumes and masks. When the masks are not being worn, they are ritually fed by the grandmothers, who are the custodians of spiritual life.

In this Kachina doll made of cottonwood root, yarn braid and eagle feathers, Hahai'i Wuhti stands ceremonially, and thus with full consciousness. From the gourd she offers the water of life, which she uses in the hair-washing ritual, an important element in many Hopi initiations. She often holds an ear of corn, which, along with water, is the basis of Hopi survival and ceremony. Hahai'i Wuhti is forever smiling, for she is always friendly and welcoming. The essence of unconditional love, she greets us with warmth and caring, always offering us the food, water and love of life.

MOTHERS OF THE DEITIES

MARY, MOTHER OF GOD

EUROPE, 15TH CENTURY C.E.

Mother and maiden
was never none but she;
Well may such a lady
Goddes mother be.
—ENGLISH CAROL, 15TH CENTURY C.E.

Here we have a French woodcarving that is a tribute to those who kept the teachings of the Great Mother alive during the Christian era in Europe. She continued to be central in people's psyches: In the early days she was worshiped equally with Christ. Later, an astonishing percentage of the wealth, energy and artistic talent of the Middle Ages was devoted to the construction, sometimes over generations, of the cathedrals of Notre Dame, "Our Lady."

At the same time, unassimilated reverence for the Goddess was threatened when church, state and the rising male-dominated medical profession allied themselves in attempts to eradicate the overlapping populations of Goddess followers, midwives, wisewomen and peasant revolutionaries. Within a period of a few centuries, an estimated nine million women, men and children were executed as witches in a suppression of matristic consciousness that continues even today.

Yet many kept the Goddess's tradition alive, both inside and outside the Church. This piece was probably made by someone who wished to portray Mary literally as the Mother of God. Closed, she is the traditional Virgin with Child. However, she may also be seen as the archetypal Mother, creatrix of life, holding the sphere of the world in her hand. Opening her reveals the truth: She contains God, Christ and the rulers of the spiritual and temporal spheres. To whom, then, are these pious worshipers offering their prayers?

Hail, holy Queen, Mother of Mercy;
Hail, our life, our sweetness and our hope.
—11TH CENTURY C.E. HYMN

41

MOTHERS OF THE PEOPLE

La Virgen de Guadalupe

NORTH AMERICA, 20TH CENTURY C.E.

*Do not be troubled nor disturbed by anything; do not fear illness
nor any other distressing occurrence, nor pain. Am I not your
mother? Am I not life and health? Have I not placed you on my
lap and made you my responsibility? Do you need anything else?*

—OUR LADY OF GUADALUPE,
ST. MARY'S CATHEDRAL, SAN FRANCISCO

One day in sixteenth century Mexico, a recent convert to Catholicism named Juan Diego visited Tepeyac Hill. Before the Spanish conquest, Tepeyac Hill had been the site of the major temple to Tonantsi, the indigenous Goddess of Earth and Corn. Juan Diego and his uncle were important figures in the worship of Tonantsi and perhaps this is why La Virgen de Guadalupe appeared to Juan Diego at this sacred place on that day long ago. She told him that she loved the people very much and wanted to protect them, and so she asked him to have a new church built for her on that site. Juan protested that no one would believe he had seen her. Mary pointed, and suddenly among the cactus grew roses, the flower of the heart and of her love for humanity.

Juan gathered up the roses in his cloak, and going straight to the bishop, he unrolled his garment. An even greater miracle appeared: An image of the Virgin as a pregnant, dark-skinned Indian woman was painted on the cloth. With stars on her cloak and a crown on her head, and the moon supporting her and the rays of the sun surrounding her, truly she was the Queen of Heaven.

To this day, La Virgen de Guadalupe is portrayed as she appeared to Juan Diego. Full of compassion, she offered a refuge from the new, angry Christian God, and by extension from the early European invaders. Adopted as Mexico's patron saint, she became a symbol of freedom from continued foreign intervention. Like Tonantsi and the Virgin Mary, who are both called "Our Mother," she embodies unconditional mother love. She does not demand penance, for she is always forgiving. Our Lady of Guadalupe is virgin in the original sense of the word, "whole unto herself." Her feast day in December is the most widely celebrated in Mexico, a tribute to the survival of the compassionate Goddess.

 *Close your eyes, and imagine that you go to your favorite sacred site or natural
setting. Allow yourself to rest there for a while, letting yourself relax into the
spirit of the place. Suddenly the Goddess, as you know her, appears. What does she
look like? How is she dressed? What does she have to say to you? Ask her what she
would like you to do in the world to help make her presence better known . . . Request
a gift from her to help you fulfill her wish. When you are ready, thank her for all she
has given you, and say goodbye. Slowly bring yourself back to your everyday reality,
carrying with you the presence of the Goddess.*

MOTHERS OF THE PEOPLE

GUANYIN

ASIA, 11TH—EARLY 12TH CENTURIES C.E.

In the lands of the universe there is no place
Where She does not manifest Herself. . .
Compassion wondrous as a great cloud,
Pouring spiritual rain like nectar,
Quenching the flames of distress!
—THE LOTUS SUTRA

Guanyin (Kuan Yin) is the most universally beloved of Chinese deities. As the *Bodhisattva* of Compassion, she hears and answers the cries of all beings. In popular conception, Guanyin went through a long and interesting transformation from male to female (see Text Notes). In this beautifully powerful, androgynous statue of painted wood, she is in the "royal ease" posture: seated, but about to rise to help those in need. In other images, she carries the pearl of illumination or pours a stream of healing waters from a vase, blessing her devotees with physical and spiritual peace. Numerous legends recount the miracles which Guanyin performs to help those who call on her, and children may be dedicated to her by grateful parents.

Women in particular devote themselves to Guanyin. Like Artemis, she is a Virgin Goddess who protects women, offers them a religious life as an alternative to marriage and grants children to those who want them. Guanyin brings souls to the newborn and rain to the Earth. Again like Artemis, she is a deity of the wild places, often appearing under a full moon, by ponds and willow trees.

In the Chinese Buddhist meditative tradition, practitioners are encouraged to develop the qualities of Guanyin which everyone contains in potential. By meditating on her attributes and her image, we can begin to cultivate compassion and a deep sense of service. In doing this, we not only help others but also move more easily and peacefully in the world. The following meditation is adapted from a Chinese Buddhist nun's description of her own practice.

Find a comfortable position and close your eyes. Allow your breathing to deepen and your mind and body to relax. Imagine that it is nighttime and that you are on top of a hill, looking out over the ocean. The full moon has just risen and the moonlight shimmers on the water. You gaze at the moon for a long time; the moonlight is powerful but soft, and looking at it makes you feel very calm and happy.

The moon now begins to get brighter and brighter, so bright you can barely look at it. Gradually it becomes Guanyin herself, her whole body surrounded by a glowing aureole. She stands on a lotus that floats on the waves. At the sight of you, she smiles a beautiful smile, and tears of happiness shine in her eyes. Imagine her radiance filling you, her strength, her peace and her compassion becoming a part of you. If you repeat her name, your mind will be calm, and she will stay with you.

Finally, it is time for her to leave, and she becomes smaller and smaller. At last the sea and sky vanish too, and you rest in contemplation of the beautiful, empty space that is left. . .Let yourself become space. . .When you are ready, come back into your body and slowly stretch. Open your eyes and look at the world about you.

MOTHERS OF THE PEOPLE

TARA

ASIA, 16TH CENTURY C.E.

Her face is a hundred full moons in autumn,
Her radiance blazes like a thousand stars,
Dispelling the darkness of ignorance.
On Her let us meditate!

—*THE PRAISE TO ARYA-TARA*

Tara, the primordial Great Goddess of Central Asia from whom the Tibetan people trace their lineage, is now beloved by devotees around the world. Her name translates as Star and She Who Leads Across. As with Guanyin and the Virgin Mary, people appeal to her in times of great need. In particular, Tara is savior of those encountering the traditional eight great dangers mentioned in Buddhist teaching: pride, delusion, anger, envy, wrong views, avarice, attachment and doubt. Like Prajnaparamita, she is the spiritual mother of all the Buddhas.

As the Great Mother of India and Tibet, Tara is at once the fierce Goddess of the Underworld, the Earth Goddess of plants, animals and human beings and the Heavenly Goddess of wisdom and spiritual transformation. When she was absorbed into the Buddhist pantheon, she became a bodhisattva, an enlightened being who, rather than entering nirvana, chooses to remain in the world until everyone is liberated. Unique among the bodhisattvas, she vowed to always reincarnate as a woman. The story of her birth from a tear shed by Chenrezi, or Avalokiteshvara, is similar to the Greek myth of Athena being born from her father Zeus' head, in that an ancient Great Goddess is subordinated to a male deity in a new, masculine-oriented religion.

As a Tantric deity, Tara is a full Buddha, as perfectly enlightened as the historical Shakyamuni Buddha. In Tantric images, Tara's primary color is green, although she may also appear as white, blue, yellow or red, each color representing a different aspect of her powers and teachings. In this bronze Tibetan statue, she is Mahatara, or Great Tara. Jewels adorn her, she bears the sacred lotus flower and a snakelike tiara crowns her head. Sensual and dignified, her stance is the embodiment of the grace and power of free-flowing life force.

Set this image in front of you and think of what help you would like from the Goddess Tara. The Kashmiri sage Suryagupta wrote that reciting Tara's names with devotion puts an end to suffering and brings true liberation. Placing our trust in her, we find that all our desires are fulfilled. Speak or chant Suryagupta's *Praise of the Thirty-two Names of the Venerable Arya-Tara: Buddha! Emanator! Chief guide! You of noble morals! Superior one! Sole mother! Saviour! Leader! Doctor! Jewel! Bearer of knowledge! Heroine! Turner of the wheel of healthy Dharma! Sun! Full moon! Lotus! Fearless one! Very firm one! Thoroughbred! Peahen! Cuckoo! Lamp! Clear revealer of beauty! Liberator! Great-voiced one! Ambrosia! Guarding life-giver! Life-giver healing the world! Sole friend! Dakini! Way-shower! Friendly-minded one!*

CREATION

MOTHERS OF THE PEOPLE

ISIS LEADING QUEEN NOFRETARI

AFRICA, C. 1300 B.C.E.

"I am Nature, the universal Mother, mistress of all the elements, primordial child of time, sovereign of all things spiritual, queen of the dead, queen also of the immortals, the single manifestation of all gods and goddesses that are. . .Though I am worshipped in many aspects, known by countless names, and propitiated with all manner of different rites, yet the whole round earth venerates me. . .Both races of Aethiopians, whose lands the morning sun first shines upon, and the Egyptians who excel in ancient learning and worship me with ceremonies proper to my godhead, call me by my true name, namely, Queen Isis."

—APULEIUS, 2ND CENTURY C.E.

Here the Goddess Isis, or Au Set as she was known to the ancient Egyptians, leads Queen Nofretari. The scene is painted on a wall of Nofretari's tomb in the Valley of the Queens at Abu Simbel. The inscription reads: "Isis speaks: Come, Nofretari, beloved of the Goddess Nut, without fault, that I may show thee thy place in the sacred world." A millennium and a half later, Isis's worship was still strong, having spread throughout the Roman Empire, even as far as England. Yet Apuleius describes the original, predynastic Isis—Isis as the primordial Great Goddess of Egypt, mother of the deities, sun and world.

The hieroglyph for Isis's name means "throne," and the pharaohs, both female and male, claimed their descent from her. Some statues show the Pharaoh as a small childlike figure sitting on her lap, and reigning queens modeled for portraits of the Goddess. She was both mother and teacher to the rulers, as evidenced in her guidance of Nofretari. The queen, crowned with the sacred vulture, trustingly follows the Goddess, who wears the solar disk and horns of Hathor.

Isis was also revered as a savior who ensured the fertility of the land and the immortality of her husband-brother, Osiris. In the same way, not only is Nofretari protected and directed by Isis throughout her rulership, but after death she is also led by the Goddess, who is often depicted with great outstretched feathery wings, guarding the deceased.

Think of Isis as the Mother of the community, the country, the world. Stand and take the pose of Nofretari. Imagine that Isis is standing in front of you, gently leading you by the hand. In what direction does she guide you? How does it feel when your actions are infused with the vision of the Goddess?. . . What would life be like in a culture where everyone is considered the child of the Goddess, where everyone seeks to fulfill her wishes?

CREATION

49

MOTHERS OF THE PEOPLE

IXCHEL AND THE RABBIT

In the very first times both people and animals lived on the earth, but there was no difference between them. A person could become an animal, and an animal could become a human being. There were wolves, bears and foxes but as soon as they turned into humans they were all the same. They may have had different habits, but all spoke the same tongue, lived in the same kind of house, and spoke and hunted in the same way.

—NALUNGIAQ, AN INUIT WOMAN

As we have seen with Ixchel the Weaver, Ixchel is the Mayan Goddess of the moon, healing and childbirth. In this clay statue she stands in intimate relationship with a richly decorated rabbit. Perhaps they are partners in the lunar healing arts. In mythology the rabbit is a scribe who records the famous Mayan lunar calendars. Similarly, in Chinese legend the rabbit sits in the moon eternally grinding the drug of immortality. Indeed, in many cultures the moon, like Ixchel, symbolizes immortality—not as the static, patriarchal ideal of eternal youth, but in the sense of never-ending cycles of death and regeneration.

As aspects of the Great Goddess, animals are equal with humans, plants and minerals. The Goddess comprises all forms of existence, each of which is essential to the Great Whole. Revering animals and other forms of life can help us to re-establish the sacred balance of life in our environment. Animals may also aid us in our everyday lives, or in our dreams, meditations, myths and fairytales. Some Native American teachings say that, since they were created before humans, animals are closer to the Source. Thus, animals can act as allies, guides and familiars in our search for wholeness.

Close your eyes, remembering a place in Nature that is special to you. Imagine an animal coming to you, an animal sent by the Goddess. Try moving as your animal would move, feeling how it lives in the world. What attributes of this animal can you adopt that will help you fulfill yourself?. . .Ask it what you can do to help our culture remember the sanctity of all forms of Life. . .Lastly, how can you carry out the teachings of your animal in your daily life? When you are finished, thank the animal for coming to you and ask it to come back to you again in your dreams and meditations.

LADY OF PLANTS AND ANIMALS

ARTEMIS

Holy maiden huntress, Artemis, Artemis
Great one, come to us!
—CONTEMPORARY CHANT

This marble statue, probably a first century c.e. copy of an original by Leochares, epitomizes the Greek Artemis. Originally a Mother Goddess who evolved into a Virgin Goddess, she has always been associated with Nature, particularly the moon, mountain forests and childbirth. Artemis is the Goddess of the night and of magic, and the protector of all wild creatures. Thus hunters and fishers must pray to her, and later offer their first catches at her shrines or in her sacred groves, in gratitude for the life taken. In this way, Artemis is similar to other Goddesses such as the Inuit Sedna in maintaining ecological balance.

The deer and bear are particularly sacred to Artemis. An aged female is always the leader in a group of deer. Because of the miraculous loss and regrowth of their antlers, deer have long been identified with the moon and renewal. Their antlers have been worn in shamanic rituals around the world, from the Paleolithic era to the present. Bears are also animals of rebirth, for they go into deep sleep during hibernation, re-emerging in spring. They are well-known for their maternal qualities. In an important Hellenic puberty ritual honoring Artemis, young girls called "bears" danced in saffron tunics.

Artemis is a Virgin Goddess in the original sense of the word, "whole unto herself." She is free to choose lovers as she wishes. She roams the woods with her nymphs and thus is associated with the Amazons and relationships between women. Many lesbians identify with her for this reason. Artemis is also a great helper of women: In the Greek myths, she protects her mother and rescues numerous women from rape. She is also the Goddess who aids in childbirth; the labor-easing herb *artemesia* is named after her.

Take the pose of this Goddess. Imagine yourself striding through the woods, your body strong. Your right hand rests on the head of the deer companion who bounds along beside you. Your left hand reaches for an arrow, reminding all that you are the protector of wildlife and women. You are going to a sacred grove to meet with other women and animals under the full moon. Feel the power of your body. Go now and join the circle of women. What ceremony do you create to celebrate your freedom? What dances do you dance, what songs do you sing to the moon? Remember this ritual as part of your heritage as a free woman.

LADY OF PLANTS AND ANIMALS

SHALAKO MANA

NORTH AMERICA, LATE 19TH CENTURY C.E.

Sacred Corn Mother come to me
Make my way sacred, fill me with beauty
That I may bring others beauty.
—"CORNMOTHER," A SONG BY LISA THIEL

Goddesses of food—such as the Roman Ana Perenna, the Japanese Uke-mochi, and the Himalayan Annapurna—appear all over the world. Iroquois tradition honors the Three Sisters: Corn, Bean and Squash. This Hopi Kachina doll of carved wood is Shalako Mana, an aspect of Corn Mother. Her headdress is made up of rain and fertility symbols. Like other Grain Goddesses around the world, Corn Mother is often seen as the Goddess of all plants: the grasses, herbs, bushes and trees, as well as life-sustaining corn. Her exposed yoni, or vulva, links women's fertility with that of the Earth.

The Keres Pueblo say that Iyatiku, the Mother of All, gave people corn, which was her heart, when they emerged from the underworld. The womb and the heart are often one and the same: When the Mother gives her heart, she gives the fruit of her womb, the corn which will feed the people and keep them alive. In the same way, all of existence comes from the heart of the Huichol Grandmother Growth. Pueblo cultures continually recognize the importance of corn as a reminder of the source of life. A Hopi baby is given a perfect ear of white corn at birth as its symbolic mother, and the presence of a perfect ear of corn is essential to the success of any ceremony.

People who live close to the earth and are familiar with the work and time involved in gathering, growing, harvesting and hunting recognize food as sacred. It is an essential part of survival, hospitality and ceremony. Many peoples pray to the plants before the first cutting, or to animals before killing. Women sing prayers as they prepare the food, and prayers are made before eating. For food is a miracle: It grows from a tiny seed, feeding on light, water and soil until it becomes a full-bodied plant. The alchemy continues when we eat the plant, transmuting it into our flesh, blood and bones—yet another form of life.

When we as a culture revere Corn Mother, when we honor the source of our food and of our existence, when we share the harvest generously with all who are hungry, we are well fed. When we live by the laws of Nature and grow our foods organically, we consume health-giving sustenance. When we eat our food in gratitude and in full consciousness of its source, we live as part of the web of all beings, and we are continually nourished.

Before you eat, give thanks to each plant or animal that you are consuming, and to the earth, air, fire and water which created them. Give thanks to the people who raised your food and brought it to you, and to those who prepared it. Above all, give thanks to the Mother, the source of all food.

LADY OF PLANTS AND ANIMALS

GODDESS OF THE SEA

ARCTIC, CONTEMPORARY

My joy
Rises from the depths of the sea like bubbles
That burst in the light;
My song
Is a promise for the winds to carry
To everyone who lives by the sea.

—*SONG OF SEDNA* BY ROBERT SAN SOUCI

This stonecut print, "Talluliyk/Sea Goddess" is by Paulassie Pootoogook of Baffin Island, in the far northwest of Canada. She reminds us of mermaids from around the world: Tiamat, the Mesopotamian Great Creatrix Goddess of the Sea; Amana, who the Calina of South America say created the cosmos; and the fish-tailed ancestor who, according to the traditions of the African Dogon people and the Near Eastern Chaldeans, brought civilization to the people.

Sedna is the "woman of the depths of the sea" from Baffin Island. Scholars have used her name to identify the Sea Goddess honored by many Arctic peoples from Asia, Canada and Greenland. She is their most important deity, and in Central Inuit villages the woman with the most authority is known as Sedna. This Goddess controls the ecological balance and food supply of many Arctic lands. In the integration of life and death recognized by primal cultures, Sedna is also the Goddess of the Dead, who descend to her watery realm.

In many traditions, the shaman travels to the Mother of All, Sedna, to beseech her help. According to the Inuit practice, if Sedna is offended by some infringement of her rules—such as overharvesting or the killing of animals that are too young—she will deny her nourishment. In order to appease the distraught Sedna, the shaman must go into trance and journey to her beautiful home at the bottom of the sea. There the traveler must comb Sedna's hair in atonement for the people's transgressions. Order is restored and the shaman returns to the human world.

This story illustrates the direct and powerful way many primal cultures use myth to ensure environmental survival and use spiritual practices to regain equilibrium. Presently, all the world's cultures are intimately connected by the threat of environmental destruction. To survive, it is important that we reclaim the myths that remind us of our dependence upon the Goddesses who are responsible for environmental stability. We must listen to their teachings in story and meditation. We must bring them to life in us and live according to their laws, that all beings may live, grow and die in natural cycle.

Mother Sedna, embodied wisdom of the connection of life with death, let me come to know you. Let me dive deep into myself to find you, that I may return wiser than before. Teach me when to give and when to take. Let me learn what I need, and what I can do without. Help me to remember that all beings are your children and that we all live in intricate balance with one another. Speak to me of your ways, that I may help restore the planet with them.

LADY OF PLANTS AND ANIMALS

For we are all,
We are all,
We are all the children of...
A brilliantly colored flower,
A flaming flower.
And there is no one,
There is no one,
Who regrets what we are.

—RAMON MEDINA SILVA,
HUICHOL ARTIST

Mariano Valadez's magnificent Huichol yarn painting portrays Grandmother Growth, the source of all living beings. The Huichol are a tribe in Nayarit, western Mexico, known for their visionary art and their dedication to their spiritual path. They receive images in peyote trances and reproduce them by pressing brightly colored yarn into beeswax laid on a wooden frame.

Here, Grandmother Growth lies at the bottom of the painting, holding the wand which contains her heart. Eagle Mother, she who brings in souls at birth, appears at the top. These two Goddesses are the oldest Huichol deities. Grandmother Growth creates the form for the souls through her dreaming, as all growth comes from her heart: the corn; the flowers; the eagle, deer and snake sacred to the Huichol; the giraffe, kangaroo and other animals of distant lands; the central peyote plant from whom the vision comes; the snakes in the sky who bring life-giving rains; and the sun with the salamanders, who symbolize transformation.

According to legend, Grandmother Growth was the first singing shaman, and all Huichol shamans must pray to her for their power. The shamans teach the people to live in cooperation and harmony, and in particular to balance female and male energies.

Different Huichol people identify with different deities, all of whom must cooperate to secure the harvest. All of their art has a sacred purpose. The women make the pottery, weaving and beadwork. Their designs come to them in dreams or visions. A woman will then make a piece of art to remember what she learned from the spirit helpers, furthering her meditation and helping her manifest it in her daily life.

Sit comfortably and place one hand over your heart. Sense its delicacy and strength. Some teachings say that the mind is in the heart. Imagine this possibility. . .As you exhale, begin to send your breath out through your heart, and gradually let it become sound. You might actually feel the vibrations in your chest. . .Still sounding with each exhalation, imagine a new world issuing forth from your heart. Send forth a vision: of viable communities. . .clean oceans full of healthy sea creatures. . .satisfying work for all. . .art, dance and song. . .loving relationships. . .and peace throughout the world. When you are finished, give thanks to your heart.

LADY OF PLANTS AND ANIMALS

PART TWO:

TRANSFORMATION

It's the blood of the ancients that runs through our veins
And the forms pass, but the circle of life remains.

—"BLOOD OF THE ANCIENTS",
Lyrics by Ellen Klaver
Music by Charlie Murphy

She changes everything She touches and
Everything She touches, changes.

—"KORE," A Chant by Starhawk

T R A N S F O R M A T I O N

*Dakini holding a skullcap symbolizing transformation.
Nepal, 17th–18th centuries c.e.*

Transformation and transmutation are essential aspects of the Goddesses of creation and celebration. For nothing is created anew: We and all of existence are composed of elements of previous life forms which have been rearranged and reordered to create new entities. Plants feed on sunlight, the nutrients of the decomposing earth and the carbon dioxide we exhale. We and other animals feed on the plants, and some animals eat other animals. Our bodies are made to decompose and create food for other life. This never-ending process is part of the continuous cycle of birth, death and rebirth that we call life. When I speak of rebirth I do not imply a specific theory of reincarnation. However, we need only look at the cycles of Nature to see that physical substances die to feed new life. Similarly, on a psychic or psychological level, we must let go of the old to create room for the new.

By "death" I do not mean simply death of the physical body. We also experience the "little deaths" of our transformations of identity, behavior patterns, home, relationships, jobs. I often use this term to describe such transitions because in accepting physical death, we can learn to benefit from transformation on all levels. Spiritual practices offer the possibility of letting old parts of ourselves die, that there may be room for new growth. Once we have learned to healthfully express our egos, we can move beyond them and feel ourselves as part of the larger life force.

I speak here of natural death, not the unnatural mass extinction that we have set in motion on the planet at this time. Natural extinctions have occurred on Earth roughly every twenty-six million years. We should have another twelve million years left of this cycle, if we do not destroy our world prematurely. Accepting our individual mortality is an important part of allowing our planet to fulfill her natural cycle. Ironically, our own fear of death and loss of possessions may lead us to destroy ourselves in a nuclear war, as we project our fears onto the "other" or "enemy." Our lack of spiritual foundation and our anxiety about material security lead us to environmental catastrophe as we drain the Earth of her resources. In addition, our fear of psychic death keeps us from acknowledging transitions in our lives or extra-rational forms of consciousness, such as the wisdom of ritual, meditation, trance and dreams.

In Euro-Western culture, which does not generally recognize or value the great interrelatedness of the web of life, and which primarily views people in terms of personal identity or material reality, transformation can be a terrifying process. We resist, dread or ignore all kinds of change, whether they be life transitions, altered states of consciousness, loss or death. We forget that, as surely as spring follows winter, new life grows out of the old. The process of letting go and emptying is essential for renewal.

Transformation is an essential part of our existence. When we die, life goes on; our individual selves do not. Many people of primal cultures, like those of the Goddesses presented in this book, who live closer to the cycles of our planet, know that death is not the opposite of life, but a gateway, just as birth is. In the words of a Pueblo Indian, "Death is a natural and necessary phenomenon, for if nobody died there would soon be no room left in the world." Similarly, on a psychic level, to whom should we offer those outdated, limited parts of ourselves? Surely not to a Goddess of fertility and abundance who would cause them to proliferate, but to a Goddess like Kali or Coatlique who has the capacity to consume that which no longer bears fruit and to transmute it into new life.

Physical death is one of the great mysteries of life, as great a miracle as birth and sexuality. When we die, our vastly complex bodies disintegrate and "we" seem to disappear. Who are we? Where do we come from? Where do we go? These are questions which challenge many of us. At both birth and death, we enter what some Native Americans call the Great Mysterious. We cannot know our future in either transition, but we *can* learn to trust the process.

In my research, I have found that *all* Goddesses of Death, taken in their original or cultural context, are also Goddesses of Rebirth, for the two concepts are inseparable for those who understand the laws of Nature. It has been frequently noted that the death throes are similar to those of birthing. Also, women have been the primary caregivers for the dying, who are often held as a child would be. In myth and art throughout the world, Goddesses teach the mysteries of death and rebirth and receive the dead back to their breasts or into their wombs. Death and birth images are often juxtaposed, for both are aspects of the all-encompassing Mother of Life. Death is not a final ending, but a return to the Mother, another cycle in the spiral of life, a doorway to another part of existence.

This concept is difficult to comprehend in our dualistic world, which has isolated and resisted the death aspect. Furthermore, in the suppression of women the patriarchy has relegated death and all that it deems fearsome (including the power of the Earth and of women) to what are known as the Dark Goddesses. Yet these Goddesses were once part of the whole, the Great Goddess, who encompasses all aspects of life. It is this split which drives us to madness and causes us to destroy ourselves and our world. We are caught in a self-defeating struggle against the very nature of life itself.

Rites of passage often imitate the processes of death and birth, for they are created to help facilitate change from one form, physical or psychic, to another. Thus initiates from around the world are known as "the twice-born." Most of us do not have ceremonies or support for changes in our lives or for confronting death. We can carry our fear and sorrow everywhere we go, until we ourselves die. Elisabeth Kubler-Ross, pioneer in working with death and dying, focuses on helping people complete their "unfinished business" concerning the deaths in their lives.

It is the same with the little deaths: We hold onto relationships, past opportunities, possessions and patterns of thinking and acting even when their vitality or appropriateness are long past. We are like deciduous trees clinging to our leaves, denying ourselves the opportunity for compost for new growth. In order to grow we must allow transformation. In order to be reborn, we must allow death.

The Goddesses of Transformation can help us reclaim the sacred dimensions of trance, meditation and creativity. To employ such extra-rational parts of our consciousness, we must temporarily expand beyond our egos and exclusively rational thought. On both physical and psychological levels, we must know death before we can lead others to life. Once we have gained a depth of understanding from this intuitive perspective, we can call in our rational faculties to implement our inspiration. In this way we function with all our resources— including our whole brains and souls united with our minds and hearts.

The Goddesses of Trance in this section help us remember our heritage of larger consciousness, embodying for us a diversity of practices: silent meditation, ritual, chanting, dreams, dance and shamanic journeying. Trance may also be a rehearsal for death, a way to practice letting go of our egos in preparation for the physical passage.

Women might have easier access to what we call altered states of consciousness, while balancing them with a practical outlook. Perhaps male initiation rites are often emphasized more than women's because men do not experience the same intense transformations that are a natural part of women's lives. In fact, many initiation rites specifically imitate women's bleeding and birthing. Perhaps the dramatic physical changes of menstruation, pregnancy, multiple orgasms, nursing and menopause are women's training for moving in and out of different states of consciousness.

We have much to learn from the Goddesses of Transformation and from peoples who ceremonially honor the cycles of life's transitions. As demonstrated in the stories of Persephone, Inanna, and the Dzonokwa, it is only by going into the underworld of our psyches that we can discover and bring back the jewels of wisdom hidden there. Remembering the unity of birth, death, and rebirth can help us heal our fears and the destructive tendencies which result from those fears. We can then truly rediscover how to live in more peace and harmony on this planet, as those honoring the Goddesses of Transformation have done for millennia.

Winged Isis, Egypt, 600 b.c.e.

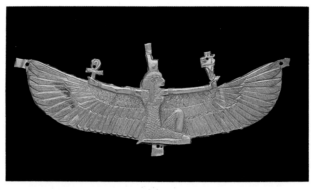

ADITI

I am the Absolute.
From me has proceeded the world of substance
and of consciousness,
the void and all phenomena.
I am bliss and non-bliss...
I am the entire world...
I am unknown.
Below and above and around am I.

—DEVI UPANISHAD

This brass sculpture from Andhra Pradesh, India, represents Aditi, the Hindu Goddess of the Void. Her name means "abundance" and "creative power" in Sanskrit. The image of any of her manifestations can be hung from the two hooks in the central empty space, just as we project various forms of reality onto the Ultimate Void.

Aditi is the primordial space, the womb from which all creation arises. She is also infinite time, a guardian of the cosmic order. She has no mother; indeed she was never born, for she herself is the origin of all. As the Source, Aditi is sometimes depicted as the Fulfiller of Desires, the Perfumed One, the Cow of Plenty, who feeds deities, humans and spirits from her great teats.

The female has been associated with the Void throughout the world, reflecting our origin in the dark creative chaos of our mothers' wombs. Since Euro-Westerners have come to identify primarily with material reality and the accumulation of goods, we fear the Void, and with it the Sacred Feminine. We have cut ourselves off from our Source, which is unknown, mysterious and full of potential. When we understand the true nature of the Void and experience its rich fullness, we learn to let go, to empty ourselves. Only then can we fill ourselves and our world with renewed life force.

Close your eyes, and imagine yourself floating in the Void, the great womb of the Cosmic Mother. It is dark, rich and boundless. If you are afraid, feel your connection to the Mother through a cord from your navel. As you begin to move in this infinite space, notice its sensuality, deep textures and velvet softness. Now you have room to stretch out, to become more of who you are...Allow yourself fully to feel that you are part of All That Is. Let yourself draw on this great source of energy. Fill your being with the life force of the Great Womb, the Void, the Goddess Aditi...Her Void is teeming with possibilities for you. Which ones do you want to touch, to take into your life? Take what you need...When you are ready to return, slowly open your eyes, retaining in your heart, mind and body a sense of the infinite resources that are available to you.

EARTH CYCLES

PELE

Then she rubs her fire-sticks to a blaze:
Up flames her touchwood, kindling the heavens.
Earth sees the flash of lightning, hears the boom
Of thunder echoed by mountain walls . . .
The firmament sags, clings to the earth;
Hawaii is lost in her smoke,
At the passion-heat of the Goddess.

—*PELE AND HIIAKA* BY NATHANIEL B. EMERSON

Pele, depicted in this beautiful painting by Herb Kawainui Kane, is the Goddess of Volcanoes in the Hawaiian Islands, and there are many chants and dances dedicated to her. Pele is one of the Ancestral Spirits who personify the life force in all its forms.

Hawaiian culture does not have a separate word for religion, and the Goddess is known to the people on a personal level. To this day, many see her and refer to her familiarly as Madam Pele. The volcano Mauna Loa is considered a manifestation of this Goddess. A Native Hawaiian group called the Pele Defense Fund works to prevent destruction of the environment—and desecration of the Goddess—from planned geothermal drilling on the active volcano.

Without Pele the islands themselves would not exist. Bringing up her great flow of red-hot magma from the deep core of Mother Earth, she created the land out of the ocean. Pele's creation and transformation of the land continue. Traditional Hawaiians, like all primal cultures, recognize that this is Pele's land in the first place and that she can take it back whenever she wants. And take it back she does, her iridescent lava—"rainbow black"—rolling down over the brilliant green of forest, garden and home.

For a while after the lava fields cool, large rick-rack spiders are their only inhabitants. They are the guardians of this sacred place, weaving the design of new life, laying the groundwork for what is to come. And then gradually tiny shoots sprout up on Pele's skin, growing to become ferns, grass, bushes and then trees, until a whole new land is created.

As befits such a powerful creatrix, Pele is also known for her passion and sensuality; the brilliant red of her lava is the color of birth, emotion and love throughout the world. Pele assumes many forms so that she may take new lovers. She can be seen as the epitome of vibrant woman: passionate, creative, expressive. Pele allows the life force to flow through her; out of a period of chaos emerges new life. It is through such passion, and such cycles, that we evolve, change and grow.

Sit in a comfortable position and close your eyes. With each exhalation, relax your muscles. Now feel a cord extending from the base of your spine, reaching far into the center of the Earth, touching her molten core. You can draw on this great source of energy. Imagine that it travels up through the cord and into your body through your spine. Let the top of your head open up and life energy fall around you in a great fountain. Feel it bathing you, coursing throughout your body, revitalizing and purifying you. When you are finished, let the fountain die down. Slowly bring your attention back up from the Earth's center, back up through the layers and back into your own body. Gently open your eyes.

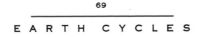

EARTH CYCLES

The Motherpeace Death Card

North America, Contemporary

We all come from the Mother
And to Her we shall return
Like a drop of rain
Flowing to the ocean.
—CHANT BY ZSUZSANNA E. BUDAPEST

Artist Karen Vogel's Death card for the *Motherpeace Tarot Deck* vividly depicts the perception of death and rebirth in Goddess-oriented and primal cultures. The skeleton rests in the fetal position under a birch tree which is dropping its leaves. Entwined around it is a snake shedding her skin.

The images in this card may arouse fear or sadness in many Euro-Westerners, but consider that for thousands of years they have symbolized rebirth. A dying person often moves into the fetal position, the body apparently recalling its form before entering the world. Beginning with the Neanderthals in 60,000 b.c.e., peoples all over the world have buried their dead in this position, some with their heads cushioned as though they were sleeping, lying on the east-west axis of the rising and setting sun. Their bodies were frequently covered with red ocher or flowers, symbols of fertility, celebration and rebirth. Sometimes they have been laid in the womblike enclosures of caves and beehive-shaped tombs. Our ancestors recognized that death was as much a part of the natural cycle as birth, sleep and the changes of the Earth, moon and sun.

Snakes have long been honored in the Goddess tradition for their wondrous ability to shed their skins without pain. They show us how to let go: Indeed, they actively participate in the process, as this snake does by rubbing against the tree. Associated with trance, snakes symbolize the "death" of the ego or rational mind which occurs when one's consciousness reaches deeper sources of wisdom. The birch too sheds its skinlike bark and drops its leaves, providing rich compost for spring renewal.

Goddesses of Death and Rebirth—Inanna, Kali, Rhiannon, Coatlique, Hecate, Persephone, Isis, Nut, Ala, Maleeoo, Hine-nui-te Po—help me remember the truth of living on this beautiful planet. Let me not fear death, whether physical death or the little deaths of the phases of my life. Teach me to accept the cycles of my life, that I may learn to release and move on without attachment. May my endings be peaceful, that my beginnings might be blessed. May my prayers and actions benefit all beings of your lands.

TRANSFORMATION

EARTH CYCLES

PERSEPHONE AND DEMETER

EUROPE, 5TH CENTURY B.C.E.

*Persephone, on her part, when she saw the beautiful eyes
of her mother, left the chariot and leaped down to run
forward. She fell on [Demeter's] neck, embracing her. . .
Thus the whole day, in harmony of feeling, they greatly
cheered each other's hearts and breasts, embracing each
other. The spirit stopped its grieving. They gave and
received joy from each other.*

—HOMERIC HYMN TO DEMETER

The Greek myth of Persephone, also known as Kore, and Demeter is the classic story of descent, death and rebirth, and of separation and reunion between Mother and Daughter. In this carving, we see Persephone holding the torches which light her way from the underworld. Her mother Demeter, Goddess of the Earth, looks lovingly into her eyes, rejoicing in being reunited with her daughter, another part of her Self. She shows Persephone a sheaf of wheat, symbol of the eternal cycles of Nature and the wisdom of matristic consciousness. Scholars believe that the revelation of the wheat was the core of the Eleusinian mysteries, founded by Demeter in celebration of her reunion with her daughter.

In the patriarchal Greek version of the myth, Demeter and Persephone live together in an eternal state of summer's abundance. Disrupting this natural matristic order, Hades, God of the Underworld, rapes and abducts Persephone. Demeter so mourns the loss of her daughter that the world begins to die. Persephone finally returns to Demeter, but because she was tricked by Hades into eating a few pomegranate seeds, she must go back to the underworld for part of each year, during which time winter reigns. Yet each spring Persephone rejoins Demeter and flowers bloom, crops grow and life returns.

According to Charlene Spretnak and others, this is a revision of earlier myths of the Goddess who chooses of her own free will to leave the bliss state of life with her mother. Some say that, like the Sumerian Inanna, she descended to the underworld because she wanted to experience another side of her Self, or that, like the Polynesian Hine, she wanted to help the souls of the dead. Others say that Persephone longed to gain the knowledge of death and rebirth from Hecate, the ancient Goddess of the Underworld.

Each version tells the story of descent into the underworld and re-emergence, both in the natural world and in our own psyches. When we explore our own psychological underworld, difficult as the experience might be, we retrieve great riches. In this process of soul-making, we can visit our depths over and over, and with each turn of the spiral, gain deeper wisdom and peace.

---

*Great Mother Demeter, Daughter Persephone, remind
me that, just as the seed must be planted in the earth,
so must I at times go to the underworld for nourishment. And let me remember that, to complete the cycle,
I must also bring my flower and fruit into the world,
that Mother and Daughter, both inner and outer, may
be reunited.*

TRANSFORMATION

DESCENT AND RETURN

INANNA

MIDDLE EAST, 3RD MILLENNIUM B.C.E.

Lady of all the essences, full of light,
good woman clothed in radiance
whom heaven and earth love...
You are a flood descending from a mountain,
O primary one,
moon goddess Inanna of heaven and earth!
—POEM BY THE PRIESTESS ENHEDUANNA,
C. 2300 B.C.E.

Celebrated for 3500 years, Inanna was the most important deity in Sumerian mythology. Originally a Goddess of the Earth and fertility, she appears in some of the most erotic poetry ever written. In time, Inanna also became the Queen of Heaven and a Goddess of death and rebirth. Later known throughout the Middle East as Ishtar, Inanna comes to us from a period of transition from matristic to patriarchal culture which began about five thousand years ago.

Here she appears on a Mesopotamian seal, her foot on a lion, her head crowned with horns, wings and thunderbolts sprouting from her shoulders. The eight-pointed star of Venus, a worldwide symbol of death and rebirth, shines behind her, while on the left a worshiper salutes her.

The story of Inanna's descent tells how she, the Queen of Heaven, decides to go visit her sister Ereshkigal, the Queen of the Underworld. Inanna counsels her attendant to send help if she does not return and ceremonially girds herself in the accouterments of her power: crown, staff, various jewels and robe. Then she sets off alone and passes through the seven gates to the underworld. She must give up one of her powers at each. When she protests she is told, "Be quiet! The ways of the underworld are perfect and may not be questioned!" Finally, naked, she approaches Ereshkigal, who "fastens on Inanna the eye of death." Inanna dies and is hung from a hook. After three days she is revived by spirit helpers and reborn.

Inanna's is the oldest tale we have of the journey of death and rebirth. It precedes and influences the stories of Persephone, Orpheus and Jesus by millennia. Like Inanna, Christ dies for three days and nights. These stories most likely are based on the fact that the moon disappears from our sight for three nights of her monthly cycle.

Inanna's story speaks to us of the tremendous power that can be gained from risk-taking and trusting one's intuition. We learn of Inanna's independence, courage, resourcefulness and, ultimately, triumph. She is a model for all of us today who seek self-knowledge, making our own personal and collective descents to the underworld.

Close your eyes and imagine yourself taking Inanna's journey. Dress in seven symbols of your identity and strength. What are they?. . .Now you begin to descend to the underworld. You must pass through seven gates. At each threshold, the guardians strip you of one of your symbols of selfhood. What must you give up in order to be transformed? Finally, naked and alone, you face the Queen of Death, and die. . .Feel old parts of yourself fall away, like a snake shedding her skin. . .After three days, spirits sprinkle you with the food and water of life, and you are reborn—yourself, but different. You rise again, ascending to the skies. You are now complete, for you have integrated the knowledge of heaven, Earth and underworld. Feel yourself in a new form, in a new way.

DZONOKWA

This wooden Kwakiutl mask portrays the giant Dzonokwa of Northwest Coast Native American myth. She is a complex figure of whom there are many stories and a variety of artistic representations. Both respected and feared, she is invoked in numerous aspects of Kwakiutl life. Like some Dzonokwa figures, this mask has facial hair. She is depicted as both intimidating and beautiful, her mouth open to make the sound of the hooting owl, with which she is associated.

Dzonokwa also signifies abundance; feasting bowls are carved in the breasts, stomach, mouth and face of large sculptures of her body, some as long as fifteen feet. She can bestow other great riches, for Dzonokwa is the custodian of valuable pieces of copper. She also plays a significant role in the potlatch ceremonies, which are important spiritual, economic, social and environmental institutions for recycling and redistributing wealth. At these rituals, the chiefs wear her masks as symbols of their power, invoking her fecundity by calling themselves by her name, which means "wild woman of the woods."

During puberty rites, girls wear a ceremonial robe patterned on Dzonokwa's own magical garments. At the same time, Dzonokwa is also the feared guardian of children, for they hear her voice at night in the owl's hooting, warning them to stay at home or risk being eaten by her. In this respect, she resembles the witch of European fairytales and the Hebrew Goddess Lilith: previously beneficent beings whose power was made malignant in the mythology of a patriarchal culture.

Dzonokwa can also be a Goddess of rebirth, if one is not afraid of her. Like many fearsome creatures, she has great riches for those who befriend her. Such stories are vehicles for psychological and spiritual teaching, for as the contemporary neopagan expression says, "where there is fear there is power." This myth of the Tanaktak people, who live at Knight Inlet near Vancouver Island, describes how one who courageously confronts the Dzonokwa learns the secrets of rebirth, both material and spiritual:

Once hunters accidentally killed the son of Dzonokwa. She was very sad and sat crying on the rocks by the river. The villagers were afraid that she would try to avenge the death and so did not try to help her—all except for one young man, an orphan who was very unattractive and seldom spoke. He paddled his canoe to the Dzonokwa and led her to her son's body. Together they carried it back to the giant's home. She gave the young man all her riches: skins, dried meat and a mask of her own face. Reviving her son with magical water, she threw some on the young man, who became extremely handsome. But he was still sad, for his parents were dead. And so the Dzonokwa taught him her secrets of rebirth. Transformed, he returned to his village, where he celebrated the first winter ritual marking the return of life, and revived his parents with the magical water. He performed the dance of the Dzonokwa and showered riches upon his friends.

Imagine putting on this mask of Dzonokwa. Feel your wild hair, your red lips and cheeks, your blue-black skin. Call the song of Dzonokwa: hoo-hoo-o-hoo. Who do you have to confront? What do you have to say to them? What riches do you gain? How can you share them?

DESCENT AND RETURN

Kali Ma

By you this universe is born, by you this world is created.
By you it is protected, O Devi. By you it is consumed at
the end.
You who are eternally the form of the whole world,
at the time of creation you are the form of the creative force,
at the time of preservation you are the form of the
protective power,
and at the time of the dissolution of the world
you are the form of the destructive power.

—*DEVI-MAHATMYA*

The Hindu Goddess Kali, whose name translates as "Dark" and "Time," is honored in India as an aspect of the Mother from whom all are born and to whom all must return. Her blackness shows her roots in the indigenous Indian culture of the dark-skinned Dravidians and also evokes her forms both as the Earth and the Womb of cosmic birth.

This gouache painting from Kangra, India depicts Kali as a beautiful young woman. Her crowned hair is full of power and vitality; her nakedness reveals her gift of truth. She dances on the cosmic couple, whose desire brings all of creation into being. In her hands she holds the sword of wisdom which destroys illusion, the scissors which cut through attachment, a severed head representing the release of the rational mind and ego, and the lotus of fulfillment. The snakes around her symbolize the transformative power of Shakti, the female life force. The arms at her waist represent action without attachment to outcome, a state of true freedom and power. Heads representing the accumulated wisdom of human existence, strung together with the umbilical cord of the soul, garland her neck.

According to Hindu cosmology, we are now living in the age of Kali. Kali energy is what moves through us in times of tremendous change, when we must face the essential impermanence of life and learn to let go. It is also what is moving through our world today, as we face the consequences of suppressing the Sacred Feminine. Sometimes this surrender is painful, particularly if we are reluctant to give up our attachments, fantasies or illusions. In fact, we might feel that we cannot survive. And indeed we—in our old forms, at least—cannot survive the changes. We must let our old selves and our old habitual patterns die, or die physically. However, when we learn to let the old ways of being fall away, we find ourselves and the world transformed, and we fulfill our true potential.

Kali Ma, Mother Kali, give me your courage that I may face my fears. Let me name them; let me offer them to you. Kali Ma, I offer you my pettiness, I offer you my sorrow. Great Mother, consume them, cut through them, burn them up. Release me from the illusions of separation and ego, free me from the bonds of attachment. Give me the power to transform my anger and frustration into clear and powerful action, that I may create healing change in myself and the world.

DEATH AND REBIRTH

Nut, Mother of Rebirth

AFRICA, 2ND CENTURY C.E.

The One of the Netherworld.
The Mysterious One.
The One of the Cavern.
The One of the Coffin.
She who Combs.
The One of the Water.
The Weaver.
—*THE SHRINES OF TUT-ANKH-AMON*
BY ALEXANDRE PIANKOFF

In this Theban sarcophagus Nut, the Egyptian Goddess of Death and Rebirth, welcomes a dead noblewoman into her arms. The image on the right represents the woman who was placed inside the coffin. When the casket is closed, both this image and her body would look directly into the eyes of the Goddess Nut (left). The symbols of the Roman zodiac surround Nut, and the scarab of rebirth rests between her feet. Her robe is decorated with the diamond glyph of fertility, water, the womb and the serpent.

We have already met Nut as the Cosmic Goddess who gives birth to the sun and nourishes the Earth with the moisture from her breasts. Because life, death and rebirth are all phases of a single, never-ending cycle in Goddess-centered cosmology, the same Goddess often stands on both sides of the mortal threshhold. In death, whether physical or spiritual, we return to the Mother who gave us life. She is waiting to comfort and nurture us, for she is the Mother who offers us regeneration. This rebirth is the promise of the Goddess.

Imagine that when you die you are received back into the arms of the Great Mother. Imagine gazing into the eyes of the Goddess, her arms raised to salute and embrace you, her breasts bared to give you sustenance in this next cycle of your existence. You have known Nut as the night sky, the constellations revolving through her as you dreamed. When you die, she takes your soul and places it in the sky as a star. Then, when the time is ripe, when you have rested long enough in her darkness, she will give you life again, as surely as she gives birth to the sun each morning.

TRANSFORMATION

DEATH AND REBIRTH

THE TOMB PRIESTESS

NORTH AMERICA, 7TH—8TH CENTURIES C.E.

The moon and the year
travel and pass away:
also the day, also the wind.
Also the flesh passes away
to the place of its quietness.
—MAYAN SONG, 15TH CENTURY C.E.

This flute-statue was probably found in a tomb on the island of Jaina, off the coast of the Yucatan Peninsula in Mexico. When played by blowing through a windpipe in her back, she covers the performer's face as a mask, so that the musician takes on her persona. Her ceremonial headdress, head covering, *huiple* dress, and heavy necklace and bracelets indicate her status. The jewelry might also have been used to calculate cycles of the moon, fertility and other important aspects of the complex Mayan calendar.

Peoples around the world and throughout time have buried female figurines with their dead as a prayer to the Goddess to receive her children back into her womb. Thousands of these statues, affirmations of the continuity of life, have been found in graves as far apart as the Mediterranean and precolumbian America.

Imagine this Priestess leading a ritual of rebirth. Her feet firmly planted on the ground, her symbols of transformative power raised high, she calls as in this song by Charlie Murphy to the spirits from all generations to help in this transition:
Calling on the spirits of the future/Calling on the lifetimes yet to come/
Send courage to the present generation/Help us find the strength to carry on./
Calling on the spirits of the ancients/Calling on the wise ones of the past/
Illuminate the vision of the people/Help us keep our feet upon the path./
Calling on the guardians of the planet/Calling on all people now alive/
With vision of the past and memory of the future/Claiming our power to survive.

TRANSFORMATION

DEATH AND REBIRTH

HINE-TITAMA

OCEANIA, CONTEMPORARY

*I will wait at this side of death for those who follow,
because I am the mother who welcomes and cares for those
children whose earthly life has ended.*
—"HINE-NUI-TE-PO" BY PATRICIA GRACE

Hina, whose name means "Goddess," is a complex Polynesian deity; many stories are told about her, most of them tales of the moon and rebirth. In Robyn Kahukiwa's compelling contemporary painting, she is portrayed as Hine-titama, the Mother of the Maori people of New Zealand, who becomes Hine-nui-te-Po, the Mother of the Dead. She is haloed by a spiral, a major motif in Maori carving, representing the ten underworlds. The skeleton is that of her husband-father, the fetus symbolizes her human children and the lizard is the form the Trickster God Maui took when he tried to become immortal.

Hine-titama is the Goddess of the Dawn, the gateway which unites night with day. Tricked by her father into bearing his children, she leaves the world of light for Po, the underworld. Once there, she becomes Hine-nui-te-Po, the Goddess of yet another passage: the Mother who welcomes the souls of the dead. Later Maui tries to conquer death by entering Hine-nui-te-Po's vagina. She is awakened by a bird laughing at his folly and crushes Maui between her legs.

In a Hawaiian story, Hina brings the people fresh water after going underground for three days and nights, like the three nights the moon is invisible to us or the three days and nights of Inanna's quest in the underworld.

Hina's youth is always restored by her canoeing exploits. As Hina of Tahiti, she journeys to the moon in her canoe. Enjoying it so much, she stays there to guard the people of the Earth.

As a Goddess of death and rebirth, Hina is probably as old as time. The story of her father tricking her into an incestuous relationship with him is most likely a patriarchal overlay, similar to the Greek version of Persephone's rape. The power of the ancient Goddesses cannot be ignored or denied, yet such revisions usually reflect and reinforce the social, political and economic changes in women's status. For Hine-nui-te-Po did not create death; it is part of the natural cycle and has existed as long as life has.

D E A T H   A N D   R E B I R T H

Oh, golden flower opened up
          she is our mother
whose thighs are holy
          whose face is a dark mask.
She came from Tamoanchan,
          the first place
where all descended
          where all was born . . .
Oh, white flower flowered
          she is our mother
whose thighs are holy
          whose face is a dark mask.
She came from Tamoanchan.
She lights on the round cactus,
          she is our mother
the dark obsidian butterfly . . .

          —AZTEC POEM

Coatlique, She of the Serpent Skirt, Mother of the Aztec deities, of the Earth and all life, is probably the most ancient precolumbian divinity. She has also been known as Tonantsi, Our Mother, and later as La Virgen de Guadalupe. This basalt statue emphasizes her death aspect, a common theme in Aztec culture. A headband of skulls garlands her own skull; she wears a skirt of bird feathers or serpents, both emblems of transcendence. The hands at her breasts perhaps signify blessings; in images of Kali, who closely resembles Coatlique in appearance and symbolism, they represent karmic action.

As the Aztecs evolved away from their source in the matrilineal Toltecs, their culture became increasingly patriarchal and warlike.

Nevertheless, they continued to revere the Goddess and Earth. As the Goddess who personifies the forces of Nature, Coatlique destroys individual forms of life that they might be reborn. Thus she is also described as the Earth in springtime. Like the Egyptian Nut, Coatlique is said to consume the sun each evening in order to give birth to it each morning.

The snake, her best-known form, represents life on Earth, for it lives both upon and within the ground and is always in contact with the Earth's surface. As the Aztec symbol for the feminine, fertility and the infinity of time and space, Coatlique's snake signifies the Dark Mother, the Earth, from whom all life is born and to which it must return.

DEATH AND REBIRTH

SELKET

"It is not I who utter it, it is not I who repeat it; it is Selket who utters it, it is she who repeats it."
—AN EGYPTIAN MAGICIAN, FROM THE *TURIN PAPYRUS*

The Scorpion Goddess Selket is one of four Egyptian Goddesses who guard the tomb of Tutankhamun. This statue is made of wood overlaid with gesso and gilded, and is one of the most graceful and powerful figures to come to us from Egyptian culture. Selket protects birthing and nursing mothers; she also escorts the dead to the underworld and instructs them in its customs. She was especially esteemed as the Goddess of Magic, and professional magicians considered themselves conduits for her work in the world.

As the Scorpion, Selket is associated with the autumn equinox, when she sends the sun Horus to his midwinter death and rebirth at the hands of Isis. The underworld aspect of the Babylonian Ishtar is also often symbolized by the scorpion. On the other hand, Selket could incarnate as a swallow, whose appearance was an auspicious omen. Like so many Goddesses, she has both a chthonic and a celestial nature.

Scorpions are honored in the Goddess art of Mesopotamia, the Americas, India and Egypt, and they are an ancient symbol retained in contemporary Euro-Western astrology. These creatures are feared rather than revered in our culture today, as is true of many symbols of sexuality and rebirth. We can pray to Selket to teach us how to let go of our fears of passion and transformation. She will show us the way, as she has for so many others through these thousands of years.

Selket, beautiful Goddess, priestess and magician, teach me the true nature of your magic. Goddess Selket, show me how to celebrate birth and how to mourn dying. Show me what I have forgotten—that transformation can be joyous. Let me give myself to your passion, for when I deny my feelings and do not express them, I poison myself. Help me know the transformation that comes from truly loving myself and others.

DEATH AND REBIRTH

GABON ANCESTOR MASK

AFRICA, C. 1900 C.E.

The dead are not under the earth:
they are in the tree that rustles,
they are in the wood that groans,
they are in the water that runs,
they are in the water that sleeps,
they are in the hut, they are in the crowd,
the dead are not dead.
Those who are dead are never gone,
they are in the breast of the woman,
they are in the child who is wailing,
and in the firebrand that flames . . .
the dead are not dead.

—BIRAGO DIOP

In much of Africa, death is viewed more as a transition than an ending. Funerals are often similar to initiation rites, for death is considered the beginning of another form of existence. Many of the dead are revered as Ancestors and serve as intermediaries between the living and the ultimate deity, who is distant and unknowable.

Painted wooden ceremonial masks of this type from Gabon represent an idealized female Ancestor, a beautiful young woman who returns to the land of the living to take part in funerals. She is tattooed with nine fish-scale lozenges, perhaps signifying female sexuality, the nine months of childbearing and the triple phases of the ever-renewing moon. Red, white and black, the traditional colors for such masks, have been used in art around the world since the Paleolithic era. These colors evoke the unified cycle of birth, death/rebirth and sexuality; the Triple Goddess; the moon. Bone-white is the color of healing, the spirit world and death in Africa, as in many parts of the world. White was also the color of death in prepatriarchal Neolithic Europe, whereas black was the color of life and fertility.

Female images have traditionally been part of death rituals in many African cultures, and it is natural that the female Ancestors would be prominent among matrilinear groups in Gabon. Masks such as this one are used as part of a moving and dramatic ceremony. During a funeral—at dawn, perhaps, or sunset—a figure wearing this mask appears, wrapped in cloth and moving on tall stilts. This is "the woman from the land of the dead." Dancing among the mourners, she sways as though wavering back and forth between the lands of the living and of the dead, for she is the gatekeeper between the worlds. People call to her, reacting to her presence with respect, fear and at times hostility. She has been known to sit on the ground, cradling a person in her lap like a mother holding her child, while the mourning continues around her. When the ritual is complete, the Ancestor figure is carried away.

Imagine living in a community where, as part of the funeral of someone close to you, "the woman from the land of the dead" appears. How would it feel to participate in a rite in which you were able to express the full range of your emotions? How might taking part in such a practice make your life, including your attitudes towards death, different?

DEATH AND REBIRTH

THE MINOAN SNAKE PRIESTESS

EUROPE, C. 1600 B.C.E.

In ancient China, India, Europe, the Middle East and the Americas, the snake symbolized the creation of Earth and the psycho-sexual creativity of individual females. Priestesses in many cultures learned mastery of serpent power, the enlightened use of our primal energy. It is the resurgence of this "snake power" in our time that may be the only hope for the survival of our planet.

—*SNAKE POWER* BY VICKI NOBLE

The beautiful Minoan Snake Priestess comes to us from the Mediterranean island of Crete. She is sometimes identified as the Goddess, yet it seems certain that she also represents actual Minoan priestesses performing ritual. Ceremonial in dress and pose, she holds an adder in each hand and is crowned with a small leopard. Both these creatures are associated with special vision: Throughout the Mediterranean, snakes were the companions of the oracles, who answered questions while in trance, and the leopard's sharp sight is capable of penetrating the dark of night.

This figure appears to be deep in meditation. Although she is only about eight inches high, her eyes are magnetic, filled with the power of trance. Her full bare breasts express her vibrant sexuality. Her fertility is emphasized by the bands on her robe, the millennia-old triangle symbol of the Goddess's sacred vulva.

The Cretan civilization, which many scholars consider the inspiration for the stories of Atlantis, was the last outpost of Goddess culture in the Mediterranean. Women were apparently at the center of this society, which was characterized by prosperity, egalitarian social structure and fifteen hundred years of peace. Minoan art, with its graceful, sensual depictions of the people, plants and animals of earth and sea, shows us that spirituality and *joie de vivre* were integral parts of this island culture.

Perhaps we can learn from the Snake Priestess some of the secrets of her people—how they were able to live in peace for over a millennium, while maintaining a culture that was highly sophisticated both technologically and artistically. The deep meditative capacity expressed by this figure and the other Goddesses of Trance continues to be a source of knowledge and inspiration for peoples throughout the world. It is probable that some of the answers to the success of Minoan culture lie in the Snake Priestess's ability to tap this primal wisdom and integrate it into daily life.

Stand up and close your eyes. Visualize this priestess in front of you, regal in a tiered skirt, her breasts proudly bared. In each raised arm she holds a living snake, whose sensuality and hypnotic gaze she has studied for a long time. When she is fully with you, let her merge into you. . . Allow the transformative energy of your priestess self to rise through you. Feel your connection with the powers of earth, sea and sky. . . What do you have to say to your everyday self? To the world? Open your eyes, keeping your awareness with the deep wisdom of your meditative body. How do you see the world around you when you are the Snake Priestess?

93

THE CYCLADIC GODDESS

EUROPE, 3RD MILLENNIUM B.C.E.

This beautiful marble statue comes from the Cyclades Islands off Greece. Almost all the art of this culture, which dates from 4500 to 2200 b.c.e., comprises marble female figures and large bowls, most of which were found in graves and ritual sites. Of the one in twenty figures which are male, the majority are harpists playing their instruments. While many of the Cycladic images are standing, all seem to be in meditation or trance. Like the matristic civilizations of Crete and Catal Huyuk, who also venerated the Goddess of Trance, Death and Rebirth, the Cycladic culture existed in peace for close to a thousand years.

Like the Great Goddesses of Willendorf and Laussel, the Cycladic Goddesses have no facial features, implying an emphasis on what we call altered states of consciousness. These deities are related to the death and rebirth aspect of the Goddess, since the "death" of the ego, even if only temporary, is necessary for deep meditation and trancework. It is likely that there is a relationship between this reverence for all states of consciousness and the stability of these cultures, for they would not be confined to the rational, ego-oriented mode of behavior of most Euro-Westerners.

The pubic triangle on almost all Cycladic female images is emphasized—in certain cases painted blue, as on some African images today. The interiors of the large, womb-shaped bowls are painted red, the color of the blood of life. The placement of figures and bowls in graves indicates an integration of birth and death, just as the trancelike nature of the statues implies an experience of all aspects of consciousness.

Lie down, your arms folded left above the right. Close your eyes. Imagine yourself lying in a rich bed of earth. Take a few deep breaths, knowing that there is nothing you have to do, nowhere you have to go. . . Imagine that your body begins to merge with the soil. Gradually your skin, flesh and bones dissolve into the earth, so that there is no separation. . . As the earth breathes, you breathe. . . Spend as long as you like in this deep silent repose. . . Eventually, feel that you are being created anew. Beginning from the inside out, feel your organs, your bones, muscles and flesh reconstructed, your body and psyche refreshed. . . When you are ready, stretch, open your eyes—and feel yourself reborn.

TRANCE

THE CHANTING PRIESTESS

NORTH AMERICA, 4TH–8TH CENTURIES C.E.

I am the woman of the great expanse of the waters
I am the woman of the expanse of the divine sea . . .
It's that I'm a saint woman
It's that I'm a spirit woman
It's that I'm a woman of light . . .
Because I am a woman who lightnings
I am a woman who thunders
I am a woman who shouts
I am a woman who whistles . . .
I am a woman of good words, says
I am a music woman, says
I am a drum woman, says
I am a woman of clarity . . .

—SONG BY MEXICAN HEALER MARIA SABINA

This polished ocher terra cotta statue of the Chanting Priestess comes to us from Remojadas, in the Vera Cruz area of Mexico. She wears a necklace of three bells and arm bracelets. The holes in her ears and head accommodate the feathers which were part of her ceremonial decoration.

The Chanting Priestess was made in an era when women were honored as priestesses and healers. Throughout matrilineal and even patriarchal precolumbian Mexico, female figures predominate. A number of them represent ceremonial dancers and musicians, and some of the figurines, like our Tomb Priestess, are actually whistles or flutes. The healing vibrations of sound have been used by wisewomen throughout time, including the renowned Maria Sabina, who sang for days in her healing practice.

Like the Minoan Snake Priestess, this Chanting Priestess appears to be gazing into another world. Although the Mediterranean figure is silent, the vehicle for this Priestess's journey is her voice; her whole posture is one of focused sound. What song she sang, what healing ceremony she created, we can only imagine.

Imagine yourself as this Chanting Priestess. Begin to sound on your exhalation until you feel the power of song rising in you. Let yourself sing a song you have never heard before. Allow yourself to sing your healing song: Chanting Priestess, help me open my body to the healing powers within. Let me release anything that blocks the power of sound rising within me. Help me find my healing song!

TRANSFORMATION

TRANCE

This astonishing clay Goddess from Klicevak, Yugoslavia was unfortunately lost during World War I. She dates from the Bronze Age, yet she carries the artistic heritage of matristic Old Europe (7000–2500 b.c.e.), and even of the matrifocal Upper Paleolithic era of Eastern Europe. In a remarkable example of the continuity of spiritual expression throughout most of human history, a Paleolithic artist engraved a very similar image on a mammoth tusk some ten thousand years before this Goddess was created (see insert).

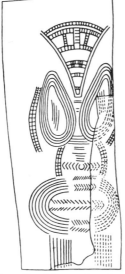

This earlier Goddess also has a bird's head, huge breasts emphasized by concentric circles and complex symbolic markings covering her body.

The story the Oracular Goddess has to tell appears in the geometric pattern on her body and the dramatic emblems of her power. As archeologist Marija Gimbutas describes in great detail, similar designs decorating Old European art associate the Goddess with birds, snakes and the fertility of rain and Earth. In cultures which do not rely primarily on the written word, weaving and ceramics have traditionally had this kind of storytelling power.

I call this image the Oracular Goddess because she seems to represent a female whose chakras, or power centers, are all receiving and transmitting energy and information. The top of her head, or crown chakra, and the bottom of her body are both wide open so that earth and sky energy flow freely through her. Snakes, identified with prophecy, spiral around her throat, and she wears the same triple necklace as the precolumbian Chanting Priestess. Her breasts and ears resemble giant receivers, while her eyes, throat and nipples are radiating concentric circles.

Like the Cycladic Goddess, her mouth resembles a bird's beak. In fact, she has been identified as an owl, the bird of wisdom. This Goddess also has a transcendent nature, beyond time and place. Embodying the power of creation by sound, singing the world into being, she is like Vac, the Hindu Goddess of Speech, or Spider Woman, who bring the named world into existence through the very power of their song and words. Once again, the Goddess of Trance is the bringer of knowledge from other realms.

Imagine that you are this Goddess from thousands of years ago. You are wearing a robe encoded with the stories of your people and their lives. You are the oracle, the trance speaker. Energy from your breasts radiates into the universe, sending and receiving wisdom. Your ears can hear everything; your eyes see all. Snakes spiral around your throat, your oracular center, which is pulsating like a star. Your mouth is wide open; you fill it with your voice. What wisdom comes through you for the people of today?

TRANCE

BIRD WOMAN

ARCTIC, CONTEMPORARY

Ho-he, aya.
Ho-he, aya.
Gull, you up there,
Steer down towards me,
Come to me.
Your wings
Are red,
Up there in the coolness.
Aya-ya,
Aya-ya.

—NETSILIK INUIT SONG

This Inuit black/green stone carving by Lukasi Uitanga portrays a woman assuming the form of a bird as she moves into trance. In traditional shamanic trance journeying, one flies up in the air or dives deep into the earth or sea. In the culture of the Inuit, which means "spirit," shamans play an important role, for they act as healers and help maintain balance in the community.

Throughout the world, shamans have been described as shape-shifters who possess the power to transform themselves. Birds have been associated with women in a sacred context from at least 20,000 b.c.e., the date of cave paintings at Lascaux, France which depict a bird-headed woman. Cranes and herons sometimes spend hours gazing at one spot, just as this Bird Woman appears to be doing.

Birds are twice-born, first from the mother and then from the egg, and thus represent the possibility of being spiritually reborn in one's lifetime. Also, their ability to fly in the air has long been a metaphor of expanded consciousness. For these reasons, shamans often wear feathers or feathered capes, carry staffs with birds carved on them or appear themselves as birds.

A Mediterranean legend says that priestesses watching cranes in their mating dance were inspired to create the form of the labyrinth, one of the most powerful and universal symbols of transformation. In rituals of renewal, peoples around the world have walked, run or danced the labyrinth in imitation of the birds' trance-inducing dance.

Imagine becoming this Bird Woman. At first you sit, brooding. . . Now let your shoulders expand into wings, your feet become claws. Your eyes are transfixed, focused on your inner vision. You begin to spread your wings. Take flight. Go higher in the sky. . . higher. . . higher. What do you see? Can you feel the wind rippling your feathers? From this height, how does your life look?. . . How does the planet look? From your soaring perspective, send healing to any parts of your own life and any parts of the globe that may be in need. When you are ready, come back down to the ground. Let your wings become shoulders again; claws return to feet. Returning fully to the Earth, retain the wisdom of your bird-vision.

TRANSFORMATION

TRANCE

THE GELEDE MASK

AFRICA, 20TH CENTURY C.E.

*"Say, for my glory, exactly
what the drums say and end it well."*
—THE MOTHERS

The Yoruba people of Nigeria and Benin make beautiful painted wooden masks such as this one for their *Gelede* performances in honor of The Mothers. There are many types of Gelede masks, some as high as three feet and weighing close to a hundred pounds. The decoration of their superstructures is inspired by everyday or mythical scenes. Scholars are uncertain of the precise meanings of the symbols on this mask, but the beatific expression and the explosion of plant and animal life seem to celebrate women's and Earth's fecundity.

In Africa, masks are made as a ritual act and have magical properties. They connote power, in earlier matristic cultures sometimes specifically the power of women. The matrilineal Baule of the Ivory Coast use female masks in their enthroning ceremonies to demonstrate the origin of the chief's authority in the historical ancestor Queen Aura Pokou. A myth of the Kono of Guinea describes how the women originally held power through their ceremonial masks. When the women lost their masks to the men, they lost their power as well.

In the corresponding Yoruba tradition, men perform Gelede dances to appease The Mothers, who represent women—especially elderly, ancestral or deified women. The name "Gelede" derives from descriptions of the movements of the *Orisha* Yemaya or Yemoja, Goddess of the ocean, the womb and women's affairs. Women are considered to have special power, called *ashe*. The focus of the ceremony is to direct this energy to beneficial ends. The leader is called Iyashe, the "mother who has the vital force."

The clothing, dancing and music of the Gelede rituals are designed with much creativity, craftsmanship and expense to attract and please The Mothers. The men wear masks, voluminous women's clothing and iron anklets with bells. They dance so that their anklets make music in rhythm to the drums. The drumming and anklet music end at precisely the same time, as described in the instruction at the beginning of this text.

The Gelede dances and the *Efe* ceremonies which precede them serve as reminders of moral order and expressions of social and political criticism. Art, music, costume and dance are integrated in a celebration and invocation of the magical powers of The Mothers, who may be called upon to promote justice and punish wrongdoing. Honoring The Mothers maintains the social order and ensures the fertility of humans, plants and animals.

TRANSFORMATION

THE DREAMING GODDESS

This sweet Goddess made of clay is one of many such statues from an elaborate system of Goddess temples on the island of Malta off Sicily. She was found surrounded by offerings. She sleeps in the pose recommended for Tibetan dream yoga—on her right side, with her hand under her head. There are similar reclining women in the Upper Paleolithic cave of La Magdeleine in France, where they were carved into the rock on either side of the entranceway.

Some of the Goddess's temples on Malta are underground, with a series of more than twenty natural and human-made caverns, carefully shaped, rounded and painted red. Niches were carved in the chambers and used for either sleeping or burial. They were probably part of a ceremony of dream incubation, a practice which survives in the Mediterranean today. Petitioners might purify themselves, make a pilgrimage to the Goddess's temple and pray for a healing dream. Tended by priestesses and priests, the supplicant could emerge with insights and healing from the Goddess.

Dream incubation is an ancient art which has been practiced all over the world—by Native Americans, Tibetans, Malaysian Senoi, ancient Egyptians and Greeks and contemporary Indians. It actively unites our conscious and unconscious minds, in order to gain the wisdom of the superconscious. "The sleep of the Goddess" is a classic description of a shamanic journey; in such conscious dreaming practices, we enter into the dark unknown to bring its treasures back into our daily waking lives.

Located at the focal points of particular Earth energies or ley lines, certain sacred sites have been considered especially favorable for tapping our deeper wisdom. The shape of the Maltese temples intensified the experience, for they were made in the form of the Goddess's body, with her womb as the ritual inner chamber and her vaginal opening the entrance and exit. Thus the petitioner could have the experience of ceremonially giving up the old self, or dying, and being reborn with new wisdom from the Goddess.

Choose an important question in your life. Think of what you would like to ask the Goddess to help heal...Every night for a week or a month, take time to focus on your question before you go to sleep. When you get into bed, take the pose of the Dreaming Goddess, resting on your right side, your hand under your head. Imagine yourself in the Goddess's temple, deep underground, united with the Earth...Ask her to bring you a healing dream. Allow your breath to center on the front of your throat, the oracular point, with your jaw relaxed. Continue to breathe, focusing on your question, and on your throat...Breathe...Allow yourself to enter the dream of the Goddess.

PART THREE:

CELEBRATION

*From Pure Joy springs all creation;
by Joy it is sustained, towards Joy it
proceeds and to Joy it returns.*
       —*TANTRA ASANA* By Ajit Mookerjee

*Sing, feast, make music and love, all in My presence,
for I am the ecstasy of the spirit and joy on earth. For
My law is love unto all beings. I who am the beauty
of the green earth and the white moon among the stars
and the mysteries of the waters, I call upon your soul
to arise and come unto me. For I am the soul of nature
that gives life to the universe. From Me all things
proceed and unto Me they must return. Let My worship
be in the heart that rejoices, for all acts of love and
pleasure are my rituals. Let there be beauty and
strength, power and compassion, honor and humility,
mirth and reverence within you. And you who seek to
know Me, know that your seeking and yearning will
avail you not, unless you know the Mystery: for if that
which you seek, you find not within yourself, you will
never find it without. For I have been with you from
the beginning, and I am that which is attained at the
end of desire.*

       —*THE CHARGE OF THE STAR GODDESS,*
       Adapted from Doreen Valiente

Apsara. Angkor Wat, Cambodia, c. 12th century c.e.
Photograph by Wim Swann.

The essence of the Goddess is joy and love of life, particularly life as we experience it through the Earth and her cycles. The sight of sunrise or sunset reflected in water, the smell of gardenias, a loved one's touch, the music of windchimes, the taste of the first ripe fruit—all these are part of our birthright, our natural heritage. So also is pleasure in simply existing, in enjoying the small and large movements of our bodies, in everyday tasks as well as in exuberant dance. One of the reasons animals are so important to us is that they remind us of the joy of living and of natural movement.

When we live close to Nature, when we are not cut off from or afraid of life, we feel our true identity as part of the vast web of being. Then we experience the true nature of the erotic, the life force flowing through us and all of creation. I use the term "erotic" as defined by poet Audre Lorde: "an assertion of the life force of women; of that creative energy empowered, the knowledge and use of which we are now reclaiming in our language, our history, our dancing, our loving, our work, our lives." Our eroticism can express itself in a variety of ways, in our passion for life, for a project or for a person. Living erotically is being open to life in all its manifestations. Living erotically is being alive.

This openness to life is beautifully expressed by Luisah Teish. Speaking of the Orisha Oshun, Teish says:

With Her we learn to love ourselves. We paint ourselves as brightly as the birds that fly. Through Her we learn to love the gifts of the Earth, brass and amber, and to become one with them. We place them on our bodies and share substance with them through our sweat. She brings us in contact with the essence of flowers. We make perfume and become one with the plant spirits by rubbing them on our bodies, into our skin. They are absorbed in our pores and we make love to them and with them...Our mouths utter sounds, we cry out ancient rhythms, haunting and sweet. We feed the hunger, heal the wounds, and give birth to outrageous beauty.

The power of the erotic is acknowledged in many cultures. *Shakti* is the Sanskrit term for the female life force from which all existence originates. Sexuality, an important expression of this life force, may be expressed in a great variety of ways. We can be sexual alone or with other people or with Nature herself. Depending on the culture, we are sexual in order to share love, give and receive pleasure, communicate deeply with one another, make babies, connect with spirit, make art, change the weather or generate healing power.

When we are able to feel the life force flowing through us and all of creation, we recognize our true nature and are able to free ourselves from the narrowness of our usual limited, alienated viewpoint. The suppression of our expressions of shakti and female sexuality has been an integral part of woman's political, economic and social exploitation. Women who fully and freely express their sexuality are, in the patriarchy, termed promiscuous, wanton or lascivious. The other extreme is represented by a thirteenth century Hindu writer who stated that a woman's virtue is proportionate to the number of lovers she has had. Either way, women are constrained by "ideals" set up and enforced by others.

The story of the exile of Lilith for her sexual independence is emblematic of the Judeo-Christian suppression of women. Similarly, in an Australian Aboriginal story women originally held all power because they were the keepers of ritual as well as the most sacred object, a representation of the womb of the Great Mother Waramurunnggoindju, until it was stolen by the men. In the Aboriginal Djanggawo myth, the females, who have clitorises so long they drag on the ground, are the most active characters. Eventually the men steal the women's sacred objects and, winning power, shorten women's genitalia.

The link between violence against women, particularly sexual violence, and the destruction of the natural world is shown in the myths of the Greek Goddesses Persephone and Demeter and of the Japanese Sun Goddess Amaterasu. Interestingly, in both of these myths it is the erotic humor of the aged Crone Goddess which lures the Earth and Sun Goddesses back to the world, that life might continue.

In Euro-Western culture, celebration and pleasure have been denigrated and relegated to so few areas of life that their remaining expressions have become overloaded and distorted. No one area of life can channel all our creative life force. For instance, sexuality cannot fulfill all our desire for or all our expressions of the erotic. As a result, our sexual relationships tend to become unsatisfying, obsessive and addictive. Only when we are freely creative in all parts of our lives can our sexuality be fulfilling. Yet as we see with many of the Goddesses of Celebration, sexuality, when regarded as sacred and as part of the worship of the whole of life, can be an important avenue to wholeness.

The eroticism of many of the images in this book might seem incongruous to those who separate sexuality from spirituality. As with other forms of celebration, our culture approaches sexuality in a dualistic way by isolating it from spirituality and either obsessing about it or rejecting it. The Goddesses of Celebration embody a sexuality which is fully integrated into the rest of reality. They teach us the wisdom and necessity of allowing the life force, including sensuality and sexuality, to flow freely. I feel that we can survive only if we honor such sacredly erotic Goddesses— and Gods. For as long as our belief systems reject the body and sexuality, we will continue to systematically destroy the world-body in which we live.

Other stories in this book celebrate the passion and life-force of the Goddess and the integration of sexuality with death and rebirth. The legends of the Sumerian Inanna tell of her descent, death and re-emergence. Significantly, her songs also contain some of the most erotic, female and eros-positive literature known. They also describe her as the patron Goddess of masturbation and, as Starhawk points out, the words of her female attendants reflect the women's intimate and possibly sexual relationship with the Goddess's body.

We can help restore the life-force on the planet by honoring sexuality—in particular, female sexuality—and all other forms of celebrating our life here on Earth. Re-establishing the sacred in life is an inevitable part of this process, for when we revere the erotic, we celebrate the body, Nature and all of physical and spiritual existence. Interestingly, the clitoris is the only organ whose sole function is pleasure. It seems that pleasure for its own sake is an important aspect of a culture which honors women.

I have selected images which I feel are female and eros-

A circle of women dancing around a woman with a lyre. Crete, c. 1500 b.c.e.

positive, those which revere and celebrate Goddesses of sensuality and passion—for these are the very basis of physical and spiritual life. I portray Goddesses who are virgin—that is, whole unto themselves—for I believe that our sexual autonomy and our capacity for joy are a direct reflection of our spiritual and political freedom. Such sacred eroticism is an essential part of leading a celebratory and creative life. When our thoughts and feelings are aligned with our bodies and when we view one another and all of creation as aspects of the divine, then we can begin to fulfill our true destiny as celebrants of the Earth.

THE COSMIC YONI

INDIA, 19TH CENTURY C.E.

She is Light itself and transcendent.
Emanating from Her body are rays in
thousands—two thousand, a hundred thousand,
tens of millions, a hundred million—
there is no counting their numbers.
It is by and through Her that all things moving
and motionless shine. It is by the light of
this Devi that all things become manifest.

—*BHAIRAVA YAMALA*

This South Indian carved wooden yoni, emanating cosmic energy, is stained red with the powder worshipers have rubbed into it since it was made. In Sanskrit, *yoni* means "womb, vulva; place of birth, source, origin; abode, home, nest; family, race, caste." It derives from a root word which means "to join together." Another Sanskrit word for vulva, *bhaga*, also means "wealth." The vulva is identified with the lotus, the flower of perfection and eternity, as well as the great cosmic void from which all existence arises.

As the sexual aspect of the Divine Female and the gateway to life, the yoni is the primary focus of worship in Indian Tantra. Hundreds of similar images appear in the art of other parts of the world, including a large number from the European Paleolithic period. Many of them have also been rubbed or handled with reverence, and today one still rubs the yoni-shaped horseshoe for good luck. The image below, from India, c. 12th century c.e., depicts worshipers honoring the Goddess's yoni.

The yoni is a primary source of life, pleasure and, when sexuality is practiced in a sacred manner, spiritual development. In Euro-Western culture, women are taught to hide their sexuality and men to fear it. To one extent or another, we have been cut off from the experience of our own vitality and pleasure. For how can we love life if we do not love the yoni, the doorway through which all life passes?

Imagine going to a temple dedicated to the Goddess. At the entranceway is the sacred vulva, the Cosmic Yoni. In order to pass through, you must first honor the gateway of life. Imagine that you take colored powder and rub it on the Yoni. Feel the mounds and folds, the strong lines of emanating cosmic energy. Make an offering of flowers and whisper your prayers to the Goddess. Let them be taken into the Cosmic Womb, to gestate and be born into your life.

THE SACRED YONI

YONI ROCKS

NORTH AMERICA, PREHISTORIC

1. *I come to White Painted Woman,*
   By means of long life I come to her.
   I come to her by means of her blessing,
   I come to her by means of her good fortune,
   I come to her by means of all her different
      fruits.
   By means of the long life she bestows, I come
      to her.
   By means of this holy truth she goes about.

2. *White Painted Woman's power emerges,*
   Her power for sleep.
   White Painted Woman carries this girl;
   She carries her through long life,
   She carries her to good fortune,
   She carries her to old age,
   She bears her to peaceful sleep.

3. *You have started out on the good earth;*
   You have started out with good moccasins;
   With moccasin strings of the rainbow, you
      have started out.
   With moccasin strings of the sun rays, you
      have started out.
   In the midst of plenty you have started out.

—SONGS FROM CHIRICAHUA APACHE GIRLS' PUBERTY RITES

The indigenous Kumeyaay of the Southern California desert used these rock formations in women's and girls' rituals. The folds are darkly pigmented, and the natural lines radiating from the vulva might have been enhanced by the people. Yoni rocks are found throughout North and South America.

A girl's coming-of-age ceremony is a beautiful and important ritual in many parts of the world. I believe that without meaningful puberty rites, we can never fully grow up. Health educator Sacheen (Cruz) Littlefeather, Apache/Yaqui, says that "traditional people around the world see the wholeness of things. Puberty ceremonies recognize the individual girl's becoming a woman as being in congruity with the fertility of the Earth and the entire female population of the world."

Among the Kumeyaay, full moon-shaped stones were used in the ceremonies, and in some puberty rites corn was placed between the young woman's legs. At puberty, a girl of the Northern California Washoe tribe would fast for four days and then, carrying live coals, climb a mountain. After lighting four sacred bonfires, she would race down the mountain to be greeted by her people with the night-long Dance of the Woman.

The contemporary Apache practice a ritual called the Sunrise Ceremony given to them by White Shell Woman (sometimes called White Painted Woman) which is symbolic of the girls' life journey. To prepare for it, the girl stays for four days in a special *wickiup*, a round enclosed structure, and is herself called White Shell Woman. When she emerges, she dresses in pollen-yellow buckskin decorated with the moon, sun and stars, the fringe representing rays of light. Now she is able to give blessings like the Goddess, scattering pollen over the people, especially the children. Great feasting, a giveaway and dancing follow. This is why an Apache girl at her first menstruation is known, according to Sacheen Littlefeather, as "she who brings forth life to our people and brings purity and beauty into our spirits."

T H E   S A C R E D   Y O N I

That Power who is defined as Consciousness
in all beings, reverence to Her, reverence
To Her, reverence to Her, reverence, reverence...

That Power who exists in all beings as Energy,
reverence to Her, reverence to Her, reverence
to Her, reverence, reverence...

That Power who exists in all beings as
Loveliness, reverence to Her, reverence to
Her, reverence to Her, reverence, reverence...

That Power who exists in all beings as
Compassion, reverence to Her, reverence to
Her, reverence to Her, reverence, reverence...

—DEVI MAHATMYA

Shakti, the active life force of the universe, is a manifestation of the Hindu Great Goddess, or Devi. She is represented in this South Indian wood carving as a temple dancer with the kundalini snake emerging from her yoni. According to Tantric belief, the serpent energy of kundalini, whose movement up the spine results in enlightenment, is already active in women. Through an elaborate process of prayer, worship of the woman's body as that of the Goddess, and finally sexual union, the practitioner may merge with the Goddess, or life force, herself.

South India, the origin of this carving, is a stronghold of the Goddess culture of the pre-Aryan Dravidians. It is likely that these ancient teachings were passed down through women. Men could gain wisdom through Tantric ritual with women practitioners. Women's relationships with each other would intensify the experience of union with the Goddess.

As we have seen, the snake is sacred to the Goddess throughout the world; indeed, in Egypt the hieroglyph for "snake" also stands for "Goddess." As the snake sheds her skin, so does a woman shed her uterine lining during menstruation. Tantric practices retain elaborate practices respecting the menstruating Goddess. For example, there is a shrine in India at a yoni-shaped spring whose water runs red with iron oxide when it is most active. This water is drunk ritualistically as the Goddess's menstrual blood.

Menstruating women have been honored throughout the world. Some scholars maintain that the first blood on the altar was menstrual and birth blood, and that blood sacrifices were instituted in imitation of women's natural flow. In some Native American cultures, a menstruating woman's dreams are consulted as important oracles. In Euro-Western society, which ignores women's menstrual cycles except as a social or medical problem, this power is distorted, resulting in physical and mental pain. In Tantra, a menstruating woman is considered to be at the height of her power. During her "red time," she becomes a true transmitter of the life force, able to act and respond with power and wisdom.

THE SACRED YONI

In the series of images on the following pages, women, Ancestors and Goddesses from around the world display their sacred vulvas. A number of these pieces are from doorways, a reminder that the yoni is the literal gateway to life. Textile scholars have shown that the Paleolithic image of the Open-legged Goddess was abstracted over time into the diamond glyph seen in Oriental rugs and other textiles throughout the world today. These figures reflect the inspirational quality of active female sexuality and power. Source of pleasure, fertility and protection, the yoni is displayed with authority and pride. The degree to which these images seem shocking or strange is an indication of how far we have come from honoring the Goddess, women and our bodies.

1. ADYA-SHAKTI
INDIA, 11TH CENTURY C.E.

According to Ajit Mookerjee, the first is of Adya-Shakti, the Primordial Ground of Being from which all existence arises. Her shape resembles the mountains and valleys of the Earth herself.

2. HERALDIC WOMAN
SOUTH AMERICA, DATE UNKNOWN

The heraldic woman motif—a woman flanked by two animals—appears in the art of every continent. In this stone carving from Ecuador, the heraldic woman's legs are open in the posture of sexuality and birth.

3. SHEELA-NA-GIG
EUROPE, 9TH CENTURY C.E.

Many churches and castles in the British Isles contain stone carvings of a type called Sheela-na-gig. This one is from the Church of St. Mary and St. David in Kilpeck, England. Early Celtic Christianity honored the Goddess: Churches had women priests, Mary was worshiped equally with Jesus and St. Bridget was acknowledged as the mother of the church. Sheela-na-gigs, with their playful eroticism, were perhaps slipped in by Goddess-honoring builders as a form of Celtic humor, or they might have been incorporated purposefully to imply the Goddess's sanctification of the new churches. Not surprisingly, most of them were removed by the Puritans.

4. ANCESTOR SPIRIT
OCEANIA, 19TH–20TH CENTURIES C.E.

The Goddess appears in many parts of Oceania. The open-legged motif, both figurative and abstract, is the dominant form in Pacific art, representing birth, death, rebirth and protection. This Micronesian Ancestor Spirit from Palau made of painted wood was placed over the ceremonial house for unmarried men, presumably to establish the presence of the Sacred Feminine in their transition from youth to marriage.

Men's ceremonial houses of the Sepik River in Papua New Guinea are built to represent the mythical primal woman. Her figure also guards the entranceway to the most sacred ritual objects: To reach them, the men must enter and re-emerge by crawling between her legs. A similar figure in another part of Papua New Guinea was hung in the men's meeting house as a reminder of a myth in which, when a woman was raped by a group of men, her spirit in turn raped the men, who died.

5. MANUBI
AUSTRALIA, 20TH CENTURY C.E.

Midjaumidjau of the Aboriginal Gunwinggu tribe made this bark painting of Manubi, a pseudo-historical woman whose sexual adventures are legendary. It is part of a series of illustrations of Manubi stories associated with sexual magic.

In contemporary life, the elder women of many Aboriginal tribes lead rituals for menarche, menstruation and childbirth, including songs emphasizing the importance of the clitoris in sexuality. In the early stages of the Djanggawo creation myth, the two Djanggawo Sisters' clitorises were so long that they made grooves on the ground as they walked, and they had to lay them on their thighs in order to reach their vaginas.

6. THE DOORWAY
AFRICA, C. 19TH CENTURY C.E. OR EARLIER

Although we have no firsthand information about this wooden door from Gabon, the diamond glyph markings are a universal symbol of the feminine, and her particular hair design might denote her status. According to scholars Vogel and N'Diaye, her dreamlike expression suggests that this was the doorway to a sleeping chamber.

1.

2. 3.

C E L E B R A T I O N

4.

6.

5.

GREEN GULCH GREEN TARA
NORTH AMERICA, CONTEMPORARY

*By taking care of our precious Earth today
we take care of our future.*

—MAYUMI ODA

Re-imaging traditional Goddesses is an important part of creating a Goddess culture that speaks to our times. This lovely silkscreen print is contemporary artist Mayumi Oda's vision of the Tibetan Buddhist Goddess Green Tara. Her name comes from the Zen center called Green Gulch Farm in the San Francisco Bay Area, whose garden is renowned for its beautiful vegetables and flowers. As Lady of the Plants and Animals, Tara has often been depicted in a special forest; she is more closely linked with the outdoors and Nature than any other Buddhist deity except Guanyin.

In a celebration of the sacred life-bestowing powers of plants, Green Gulch Green Tara sits on a huge cabbage throne while sweetpeas dance around her. At one with the cycles of Nature, she is in the traditional pose of a bodhisattva about to rise to help those in need. Her right hand gives blessings and her left holds a sweetpea vine. At her feet are the three jewels of Buddhism: *buddha* (the awakened mind), *dharma* (the teachings) and *sangha* (the community).

As a bodhisattva, Tara is a fully awakened being who, rather than dissolve into bliss, has chosen to reincarnate and work for the liberation of all beings. Inspired by a love of Nature and all her creatures, many of us have taken this bodhisattva vow, whether formally or informally, consciously or unconsciously. In our time, however, the immediate concern is with survival as well as enlightenment.

When we remember that we are part of the web of life, we realize that the condition of every living being affects us. This awakening is the essence of true spirituality and a guarantee of political and social consciousness. To the degree that we recognize and feel, on a visceral level, the joyful truth of our interconnectedness, we commit ourselves to personal and global salvation.

Green Gulch Green Tara's eroticism is an important aspect of her bodhisattvahood: The sweetpea represents the yoni, and she is surrounded by the sensual abundance of Nature. One of Tara's human incarnations was as the Tibetan mystic Yeshe Tsogyal, who helped many people to full enlightenment through sacred sexual union with her.

---

*Homage to Tara our mother:
great compassion!
Homage to Tara our mother:
a thousand hands, a thousand eyes!
Homage to Tara our mother:
queen of physicians!
Homage to Tara our mother:
conquering disease like medicine!
Homage to Tara our mother:
knowing the means of compassion!
Homage to Tara our mother:
a foundation like the Earth!
Homage to Tara our mother:
cooling like water!
Homage to Tara our mother:
ripening like fire!
Homage to Tara our mother:
spreading like wind!
Homage to Tara our mother:
pervading like space!*

—TRADITIONAL TIBETAN PRAYER

Green gulch Green Tara   29/45   Mayumi

THE SACRED EROTIC

VAJRAVARAHI

ASIA, 17TH CENTURY C.E.

OM! Veneration to you, noble Vajravarahi!
OM! Veneration to you, noble and unconquered!
  Mother of the three worlds! Mistress of knowledge!...
OM! Veneration to you, Vajravarahi! Great yogini!
  Mistress of love! She who moves through the air!

—TIBETAN TEXT

This is a bronze statue of Vajravarahi, one of the Dakinis (Tibetan: *Khadro-ma*, sky-goer) of Tibetan Tantric Buddhism, which derived from Indian matristic cultures. Dakinis are Goddesses who may manifest themselves on a human level and their teachings are conveyed in the mysterious script of the "twilight language." Tantric women practitioners are known to transmit their wisdom energy in everyday life, as well as through sexual relationships.

Dakinis teach us about fire energy and how to dance with it. In Vajravarahi, the wrathfulness (which cuts through ignorance) and compassion of her face are united with the sensuality and passion of her body. She holds the knife of insight and the skullcup of blood, symbolizing the vagina containing the potential for new life. She is crowned and adorned with turquoise. As we have seen with priestesses in other cultures, Vajravarahi's bracelets intensify the power of the movements of her arms and ankles, and her dance is accentuated by a flowing ceremonial scarf.

The Sacred Feminine is still an important aspect of Tantra and Tibetan Buddhism. Some of these traditions were founded by women, and they emphasize immanence and a delight in the world rather than transcendence and a belief that the world is evil. Instead of encouraging harsh asceticism, they teach that we are already enlightened and need only to allow our original natures to shine through. The Dakinis are our allies in this work. According to Tsultrim Allione, they represent "the everchanging flow of energy with which the spiritual practitioner must play in order to become realized. (One must) come to know the mirror of the mind, the mysterious home of Dakini."

Vajravarahi, show me how to be powerful and compassionate at the same time—let me know that these qualities are one force. Teach me to feel the beauty, power and eroticism of my own being. Show me that I am an exquisite part of the life force, dancing with all other forms of life.

THE SACRED EROTIC

THE GODDESS AS YOGINI
ASIA, 3RD MILLENNIUM B.C.E.

Look upon a woman as a goddess
whose special energy she is,
and honour her in that state.
— *UTTARA TANTRA*

All the pilgrimage-
centres exist in woman's body.
— *PURASCHARANOLLASA TANTRA*

This bronze Yogini comes from Mohenjo-daro in the Indus Valley of Pakistan, the site of a highly developed pre-Aryan matristic culture rich in Goddess art. The Yogini, probably a priestess of the original Tantric tradition, seems to radiate pride in her sacred sexual nature. Her pose is an early version of later more elaborate Indian *mudras*, or gestures; her facial features might reflect African influence on this culture.

In Tantric practice, certain dance and yoga postures along with stimulation of special points on the body enable a woman to maximize her cyclic flow of energy, affected by the dark and light phases of the moon. This is one of the oldest images we have of a woman spiritual practitioner in a tradition with which we are at least partially familiar. Women who study or intuit such practices are stepping into a lineage at least five thousand years old.

Take this pose. Imagining that you are the stately Yogini, recite the following text:

Woman is the creator of the universe,
the universe is her form;
woman is the foundation of the world,
she is the true form of the body.
Whatever form she takes,
whether the form of a man or a woman,
is the superior form.
In woman is the form of all things,
of all that lives and moves in the world.
There is no jewel rarer than woman,
no condition superior to that of a woman.
There is not, nor has been, nor will be
any destiny to equal that of a woman . . .
there is not, nor has been, nor will be
any holy place like unto a woman.
There is no prayer to equal a woman.
There is not, nor has been, nor will be
any yoga to compare with a woman,
no mystical formula nor asceticism
to match a woman.
There are not, nor has been, nor will be
any riches more valuable than woman.
— *SAKTISANGAMA TANTRA*

CELEBRATION

THE SACRED EROTIC

LILITH

Wild cats will meet hyenas there,
The satyrs will call to each other,
There Lilith shall repose
And find her a place of rest.
—ISAIAH 34:14

In this Sumerian terra cotta plaque Lilith, known as "the hand of Inanna," appears winged, taloned and crowned. She stands on her lion throne, holding the staff and circle of power, flanked by two owls. Like cats, owls are creatures of the night; in Hebrew Lilith's name means "owl." Lilith, Chokmah (Wisdom) and the Shekinah (the feminine emanation of the Divine) are all aspects of Iahu Anat, the original Great Goddess of the Semitic people.

In the Biblical tradition Lilith was the first woman, created simultaneously with Adam. In the beginning they got along quite well, but then Adam tried to force Lilith sexually. She refused, insisting on maintaining equality with him. Adam complained to God, who turned against Lilith. She then tricked Yahweh into revealing his secret name of power, grew wings and flew out of Paradise to live in the desert.

God then created Eve, who was more compliant (but still independent enough to eat of the Tree of Knowledge). Lilith remained a strong figure in Jewish folklore until the sixteenth century c.e. Originally it was she who brought agriculture to the people, she who was a midwife and a protector of children, although patriarchal myth turned her into a demon.

Lilith is particularly important because her story tells us of the essential role that the suppression of female sexuality plays in the transition between egalitarian and hierarchical culture. She cannot remain in the patriarchal order if she is to maintain her sexual freedom and equality, and the patriarchy must demonize her for her assertiveness. In spite of adversity and exile, Lilith remains independent and wild. As we reclaim Lilith, we reclaim ourselves, our bodies and our freedom.

Find a place where you feel comfortable and safe. Take off your clothes and stand or sit in front of a mirror. Imagine that you embody Lilith's independent sexuality: Feel her strength, her earthiness, her passion flow through you. How do you feel about yourself? How do you feel about your erotic relationships with others? How can the Lilith in you be reclaimed and expressed?

THE SACRED EROTIC

ISHTAR

Her lips are sweet,
Life is in Her mouth.
When She appears, we are filled with rejoicing.
She is glorious beneath Her robes.
Her body is complete beauty.
Her eyes are total brilliance.
Who could be equal to Her greatness,
for Her decrees are strong, exalted, perfect.
—MESOPOTAMIAN TEXT, C. 1600 B.C.E.

This lovely alabaster figure set with ruby navel and eyes is Ishtar, Babylonian descendant of the Sumerian Inanna. Many of their stories and attributes are the same. Like Inanna, Ishtar is an all-encompassing Goddess of birth, death, rebirth and passionate sexuality. Both are associated with the planet Venus, the morning and evening star. In addition, some scholars hold that the Biblical heroine Esther is actually another form of Ishtar. Through her associations with the pomegranate and the lily, Ishtar is also linked with Astarte, Lilith, Persephone, Aphrodite and Mary.

In the Bible, the holy sexuality of Ishtar's priestesses is denounced, and Ishtar herself is related to the "heathen" Canaanite Goddess Ashtoreth or Asherah. The early sacred sexual practices of the Goddess were an important part of celebrations that honored the female. In the transition to patriarchy, these rites were co-opted by the priestly hierarchy as they established control over the sexual priestesses, who in some cases became slaves.

If practiced with reverence, sexuality can be a joyful path to deep spiritual liberation. Each person is regarded as the actual embodiment of the Goddess. A sexual relationship becomes less an attachment to an individual person and more a meditation towards union with the Goddess.

The early rites of Ishtar also encompassed death and rebirth, for in sexuality we are born, die and are reborn. Our conception occurs in sexual union. When we make love in a sacred manner we surrender our egos, and from such lovemaking we emerge physically and spiritually renewed. In such sacred sexual practices we invoke the Goddess.

Holy Mother Ishtar, teach me to love my body just as it is. Made from your earth, I am sacred. Help me remember the pleasures of my physical being and the joys of my senses. Remind me that in the artistry of adorning myself, I celebrate your beauty. O Shining One, Ishtar, teach me to worship the Goddess in myself!

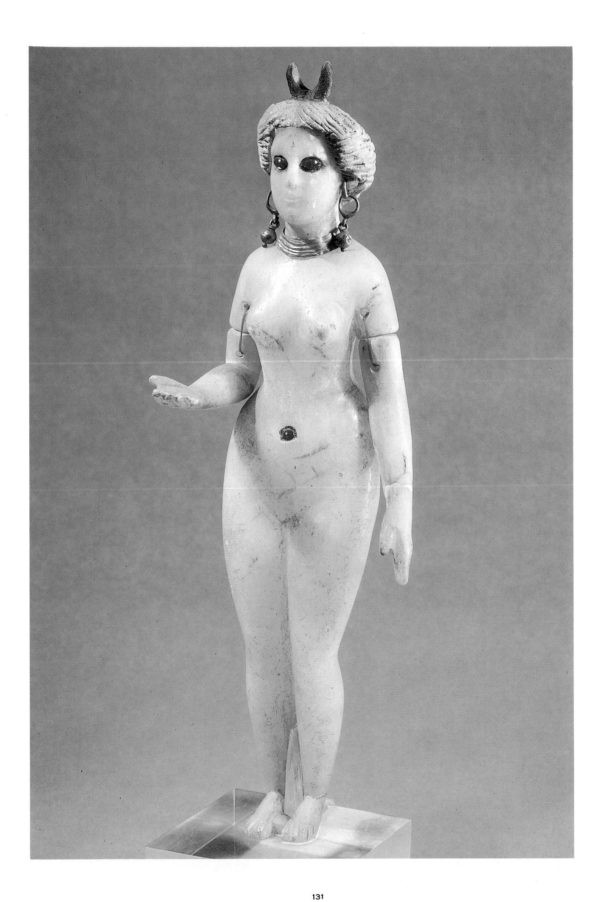

THE SACRED EROTIC

Golden Aphrodite, born of the sea, is the Greek Goddess of passionate relationships, well-being and the creative force. She is known as Aphrodite Urania, the Queen of Heaven, and Aphrodite Pandemos, Goddess of All the People. Doves and waterbirds attend her, as do the Graces, who dress her in robes dyed with spring flowers. Her particular flowers are the rose and the lily, representing the vulva; her special fruit is the apple of fertility.

Aphrodite is a Goddess of the waters, the source of life and the element linked with the emotions. She is the dew and rain which unite heaven and earth.

Aphrodite is also the Goddess of Dawn, bringing life-giving light to the world. Her beauty has a special radiant quality, perhaps deriving from this light she embodies. In a description from the *Iliad*, she presents herself to Helen of Troy as an old woman. Helen recognizes Aphrodite by the "sweet throat of the Goddess and her desirable breasts and her eyes that were full of shining." When Aphrodite enters us, as when we fall in love or are beloved, we emanate this light.

Aphrodite is an important model. She represents the transformative power of love and sexuality and our capacity to grow through joy and pleasure. She is guided by her passions, allowing them to determine her actions, yet she is autonomous and powerful.

The only Goddess portrayed nude in Greek art, Aphrodite is often shown bathing or wringing her hair after emerging from the sea. Her nakedness lacks self-consciousness, as does her attitude towards her sexuality. As Aphrodite Kallipygos, or Aphrodite of the Lovely Backside, the Goddess lifts her robe to admire her own full buttocks. In an eros-phobic culture, such self-admiration is termed vanity, yet she can be seen as life appreciating itself.

Aphrodite's passion extends to all areas of life. She loves children and laughter. We are as filled with her light when we are passionately involved in a project or experiencing oneness with Nature as when we are attracted to another person. Sometimes our attractions to people express themselves sexually, sometimes creatively, at other times in deep friendships. When we are in love with life, or any aspect of it, we shine with the light of Aphrodite.

To invoke Aphrodite's life-giving presence in your life, arrange a simple altar to her, outdoors if possible. Arrange on it flowers, seashells and any personal items which might represent Aphrodite's powers to you. Imagine that you are bathed in, and breathing in, the golden light of Aphrodite. Read aloud this invocation to her, written by Sappho in the sixth century b.c.e.:

You know the place: then

*Leave Crete and come to us
waiting where the grove is
pleasantest, by precincts*

*sacred to you; incense
smokes on the altar, cold
streams murmur through the*

*apple branches, a young
rose thicket shades the ground
and quivering leaves pour*

*down deep sleep; in meadows
where horses have grown sleek
among spring flowers, dill*

*scents the air. Queen! Cyprian!
Fill our gold cups with love
stirred into clear nectar*

133

XOCHIQUETZAL

NORTH AMERICA, C. 8TH CENTURY C.E.

. . .You alone bestow
intoxicating flowers,
precious flowers.
You are the singer.
Within the house of springtime,
You make the people happy.
—NEZAHUALCOYOTL, C. 1450 C.E.

Scholars identify this lovely Mayan clay whistle from Jaina, Mexico as a "deity emerging from a flower." The deity is most likely Xochiquetzal, or "Precious Flower," the Goddess of pleasure, sexuality, beauty and flowers. It is probably Xochiquetzal to whom Tlazolteotl is giving birth in the image earlier in this book. Xochiquetzal lives on a mountaintop with musicians and female dancers and brings good luck to children. Merlin Stone says that "when a woman felt the pleasures of her body, it brought special joy to Xochiquetzal."

Like many peoples, the Mayans and Aztecs identified flowers with song, perhaps because both are such joyful expressions of life and at the same time are so ephemeral. As with sacred sexuality, flowers and music transport us beyond our everyday concerns to our transcendent selves.

Both Xochiquetzal and this sculpture celebrate female sexuality as a source of erotic pleasure and spiritual transformation. Flowers have been associated with women and the yoni around the world. In India, for example, the yoni is described as the sacred lotus in both its bud and full blossom stages.

Xochiquetzal is a Goddess of delight. Because of her association with flowers and sexuality, she is sometimes represented as a butterfly.

Symbol of rebirth and transcendence, the exquisitely ephemeral butterfly sips the nectar of the flower, just as a woman's lover might sip the nectar of her yoni. So also, in Hindu and Buddhist texts an enlightened being sips the ambrosia of transformation.

In ancient rituals honoring Xochiquetzal, young people made a bower of roses, and, dressed as hummingbirds and butterflies, they danced around the image of the Goddess of flowers and love. The ecstatic faces of the famous "Laughing Goddesses" (see insert) from the Veracruz area were probably modeled after Xochiquetzal's priestesses.

A myth from the original inhabitants of what is now Natchez County, Mississippi, who traded with Central Americans, gives a similar picture of joyful female sexuality:

One day, the Goddesses challenged a human woman over who among them had the most beautiful pubic hair. Following the advice of her animal guardian, the mud-wasp, the heroine conjured up a hummingbird, who wove the iridescent down of her breast feathers into the woman's pubic hair. And so, with the aid of the flower-loving hummingbird, the woman's yoni outshone even that of the Goddesses, and she won the contest.

THE SACRED EROTIC

THE APSARAS

Like Xochiquetzal, the Apsaras of Hinduism and Buddhism are Nature Spirits celebrated for their sacred sexuality, music and dance. This beautiful stone carving is from the famed Angkor Wat temple complex in Cambodia, built by the Khmer people whose culture flowered in the twelfth century c.e. Of some two thousand lifesized carvings of Apsaras, no two are alike. They wear magnificent headdresses and beautiful sensual garments. Their facial expressions and the mudras of their hands and bodies are those of strong, wise, beneficent and erotic beings.

Apsaras have been compared with other Goddesses, particularly Xochiquetzal emerging from a flower, since they are frequently depicted dancing on a lotus. Lotuses are symbolic of female sexuality and eternity, for in physical joy there is eternal bliss. Like the Triple Goddess, Apsaras are of the earth but are equally identified with the sea and sky. They resemble the Dakinis in combining the celestial and highly erotic, offering the possibility of transcendence through enlightened sexuality. And, like the Dakinis and the Yogini of Mohenjodaro, the Apsaras may manifest as human women, priestesses of the sacred sexual rites.

Hindu myth says that the Apsaras—also known as the Daughters of Pleasure, the Lightning Princesses and the Cloud Damsels— live in a dimension paralleling the human realm. Born when the oceans were churned, their name means "moving in the water." The fluidity of their bodies, like the movement of lovers, reflects the undulations of the sea, source of all life.

The gentle-eyed Apsaras are described as large-hipped and slow-moving. They take as many lovers as they like, both human and divine—so many that they lose count of them. One can hear the music of their cymbals and lutes among the fig trees, where they sometimes live. Like Queen Maya, they are connected with the early matristic origins of Buddhism in Nature, and specifically tree, religions.

The power of the Apsaras and priestesses is reflected in accounts of the lives of the Khmer women. Both women and men wore a small but rich loincloth, adorning themselves with scent and flowers. Among the ruling class at least, the Khmer women were as educated as the men and known for their intellectual and scientific prowess. They served as businesswomen, professors and judges. Like the Apsaras, the women lived full, independent erotic lives.

Study these images of the Apsaras, for you can learn sacred dance from them. If you can, stand up. Place your hands on your pelvic bone. Close your eyes and begin to imagine that you can send the exhalation of your breath down your arms, out your hands and into your pelvis. Allow the muscles in your stomach, genitals and anus to relax. Feel the energy flowing down from your hands, through your pelvis and into your legs. Imagine your body relaxing and filling with a warm softness. Gently begin to move your hips, your pelvis. Let your body move you. Follow its own desire in your sacred dance.

THE SACRED DANCE

THE HORNED GODDESS

AFRICA, C. 6000 B.C.E.

The Tassili rock paintings at Aouanrhet, in what is now Algeria, were painted when the surrounding Sahara desert was green. This Dancing or Horned Goddess is one of many strikingly beautiful Goddess figures who are accompanied by images of rhino, hippo, giraffe and other animals, some of which are now extinct.

White outlines her fit, rounded body, which is painted in yellow ocher. The graceful tassles of her ceremonial clothing accentuate the movement of her arms and legs. She is surrounded by symbols of fertility: Above her, rain falls from a cloud, or, depending on the interpretation, a field pours down its grain; her head is crowned by the horns of plenty. Horns have been linked with the Goddess for millennia; they suggest, for example, the crescent moon, and the shape of the Fallopian tubes. They are reflected in the upraised arms of priestesses and sacred dancers such as this one, the Bird-Headed Snake Goddess and the Minoan Snake Priestess.

Henri Lhote, discoverer of the Tassili frescoes, thinks this Goddess might be an early representation of Isis as an agricultural Goddess, and that an accompanying female figure is perhaps the Libyan Goddess Antinea, who later became the Greek Athena. Lhote also suggests that the Tassili figures depict the ancient Amazon tribes of that area. He points out that among the present-day inhabitants, the Tauregs, the women are independent, while the men only appear in public veiled. This image certainly portrays a powerful female ready to take action.

Dance and movement are essential ways of celebrating our bodies and spirits, and they have always been an integral part of ceremony around the world. Throughout time, women have led dances for rites of passage, rain and fertility. Dance magically reweaves the fabric of life, renewing and transforming us. As the body moves, the rational mind is stilled, and a deeper wisdom emerges.

Although dance, along with other celebrations of the body, has been banished from most Euro-Western religious life, it is beginning to reclaim its place as one of the most important forms of worship. As Emilie Conrad-Da'oud says: "We do not move; we *are* movement. There is already a dance going on—a dance of myriad movement forms beyond anything we can think of."

Play some of your favorite music. Now take, or imagine taking, the form of the Horned Goddess. Feel your belly softly curving, your breasts bare, your legs outstretched. Flowing clothes decorate your body, while ceremonial tassles cover your raised hands. Around your head are horns representing the crescent moon; you are haloed by the spirit of life. . .In both small and large movements, begin to move, dancing to the rhythm of the cells in your body. Dance. . .dance for the health of the life force within you and all around you.

THE SACRED DANCE

I bow to Oshun . . .
There is no place where it is not known that
*   Oshun is as powerful as a king*
She dances and takes the crown
She dances without asking . . .
She arrives and trouble is appeased
She shakes Her bracelets to come to dance
She dances in the depths of richness
The water sounds like the bracelets of Oshun
We call Her and She answers with wisdom
She can do what the doctor can't
The Orisha who heals with cold water
We can stay in the world without fear.

—YORUBA PRAISE SONG TO OSHUN

Ochun, or Oshun, is the Yoruba Orisha (deity) of the river, love, sensuality and creativity. She is sometimes called the Mother of the Orishas. In "Ochun's Praise Song II," Afracentric visionary and initiate Asungi interprets Ochun as the Celestial Mermaid. Asungi writes:

Ochun has been compared to Venus because She presides over the arts, healing, gold, love and all things beautiful. She rests, full of self-awareness and self-love, glowing in the silver light of the moon, symbol of the feminine principle. Ochun is Mama of All Waters, on Earth and in the heavens. Her cooling waters are believed to soothe any person, emotion or situation, and She will send them to those in need.

Legend says that women learned to move by watching Ochun, the River Goddess, sway sensuously across the landscape. As virgin, Ochun is whole unto herself and free to choose lovers as she wishes. She is perhaps best known for the creative aspect of her sensuality and eroticism. This pan-erotic Goddess celebrates her physical manifestation with beautiful clothing, jewelry and other forms of adornment. We worship her when we do the same.

Take the pose of Ochun. Imagine yourself lying by the river, your back arched, your breasts feeling the ripple of the breezes over them. Allow yourself to revel in your sensuality. If anything blocks you from fully enjoying yourself, imagine that you plunge into the cooling waters of the river, washing away any inhibitions . . . Think of how you would most like to adorn yourself: What textures, scents and colors come to you? Feel the eroticism of every movement you make. You feel total pleasure in yourself, just as you are . . . Look up at the moon. See her light shining down on you, illuminating your wondrous self. Ask the moon to help your love for yourself grow. Ask Ochun to help you remember your beauty.

THE SACRED DANCE

The goddess is alive,
Magic is afoot.
—CONTEMPORARY CHANT

The Goddess is presenting herself to us in many ways at the close of this millennium. The more we invoke her, in both her ancient and modern forms, the more we sing her songs and meditate on her, the more alive she becomes in this world. I conclude *The Heart of the Goddess* with four contemporary images, a selection from a rich, newly emerging tradition. Inspired by their own experiences and the women's spirituality movement, contemporary artists are drawing on their cultural roots to re-vision the ancient Goddesses.

Gaia's Children reminds us of the importance of our sensual connection with the rest of the web of life. Kannon with the Sword teaches us to combine compassion with discrimination, while Grandmother Moon represents honoring our elders, particularly women and traditional peoples. Finally, Ochumare inspires all of us, whatever our color, nationality, age, class, religion, gender, sexual preference—wherever we are in the great range of human diversity—to create a rainbow bridge that will heal the world and ensure the continuation of life on Earth.

GAIA'S CHILDREN

NORTH AMERICA, CONTEMPORARY

All things share the same breath—the animal, the tree, the human. . .The perfumed flowers are our sisters; the deer, the horse, the great eagle, these are our brothers. The rocky crests, the juices of the meadows, the body heat of the pony, and people—all belong to the same family. . .What are people without animals? If all the beasts were gone, humans would die from a great loneliness of spirit. For whatever happens to the animals soon happens to the people. . .Teach your children what we have taught our children, that the Earth is our mother.

—CHIEF SEALTH'S MESSAGE TO THE PRESIDENT, 1854

Marcelina Martin's photograph "Horse-spirit", from her "Photomythology" series, captures the intimacy and ease possible in interspecies relationships, described so beautifully in the above text, attributed to a Pacific Northwest coast chief known today as Seattle. If we are to survive the current environmental crisis, we must remember that we are all Gaia's children—and we must act accordingly. For we *are* Nature, we are animals, we are body.

Nature is our greatest teacher. The more we learn to be at home with her, to directly feel and hear her messages, the closer we come to learning how to live as peaceful and productive co-creators with her. As we listen to other forms of life, which often know better than we how to live in harmony, we reclaim wisdom that was part of our ancestors' everyday life.

And so we must begin to develop a new relationship with other species. Humans have valued other animals for millennia for their beauty, companionship and spiritual guidance. Relationships with animals can be wonderfully sensual, and there is an ancient, special bond between women and horses. Being with an animal, especially one as large as a horse, can be a joyful union with a natural force far greater than oneself. For a young woman, riding a horse can be a rare opportunity for freedom.

That control is not an essential part of interspecies relationships is evident in this image, which, speaking in terms of Greek mythology, combines qualities of Artemis and Aphrodite, daughters of Gaia. Here horse and woman have a deep trust and understanding. Their backbones stretch out along one another's; the woman's hair merges into the horse's tail. This is an image of pleasure in the body, of deep vulnerability combined with tremendous strength in both creatures. Woman and horse become mirrors of one another's sensitivity, power and joy in life.

Imagine yourself with the kind of large animal to which you feel most drawn. Sit or lie with the animal for awhile, attuning yourself to its energies. Let yourself feel completely safe with this animal in ways you might not previously have imagined. You can be very strong in your vulnerability. . .Imagine that you travel on adventures with your animal friend. Where do you go? What do you learn about yourself and other forms of life? How can you bring this teaching back into your everyday life?

THE GODDESS IS ALIVE

KANNON WITH THE SWORD

NORTH AMERICA, CONTEMPORARY

To the perfection of her merits,
To the compassion of her glance,
To the infinitude of her blessings,
Worshipping, we bow our heads!
—*THE LOTUS SUTRA*

Contemporary artist Mayumi Oda's silk-screen print portrays Kannon, the Japanese bodhisattva who corresponds to the Chinese Guanyin, riding a dragon and carrying a sword. About this print, entitled "O Goddess, give us the strength to cut through," the artist says:

> Kannon is the Goddess of Compassion, and we as women have been raised to be kind and loving. This is very important. It is also important that we cut through the bullshit. Sometimes we have to be ruthless in order to be compassionate, to have the wisdom to know what is right action. So I have given Kannon a sword which cuts through. She is a Goddess who stands by herself, that is, on her own two feet, just as we must learn to do.

Mayumi's Kannon comes from a Japanese tradition of bodhisattvas carrying various implements or tools to help them in their task of liberating all beings. Her dragon is the protector of the three jewels of Buddhism, buddha, dharma and sangha. Kannon is surrounded by the sacred lotus in its bud, flower and seed forms, representing the three stages of the cycles of growth. She integrates the dualities of love and power, dark and light, earth and sky. The sword she carries is the sword of clarity and wisdom to cut through illusions—our own and others'.

The lesson of Kannon with the Sword is a very important one for us today, for we have confused compassion with sympathy and isolated it from strength. Too often, we think that kindness only means being nice, supportive or "unconditionally giving." However, as we can see from the great numbers of people, primarily women, now seeking to free themselves from what has been identified as co-dependent behavior, such "kindness" generally arises out of fear, not love.

When abuse or denial occurs—whether with oneself, another being, an institution or the planet—the most compassionate thing we can do for everyone involved is to name it and act appropriately. This is what the Buddhists call "skillful means." Thus we can invoke Kannon with the Sword, asking that we may embody her compassion and her grace.

Kannon, give us the courage to see ourselves honestly and with compassion. Lend us your sword, that we may cut through illusion, denial and abuse. Let us name what we see, that we may act with power and love.

146

O, Goddess! give us the strength to cut through! ³⁸/₄₅   Mayumi 真弓

THE GODDESS IS ALIVE

Surrounded by my shields, am I:
Surrounded by my children, am I:
I am the void.
I am the womb of rememberance.
I am the flowering darkness.
I am the flower, first flesh.
. . .In this darkness, I am
Turning, turning toward a birth:
My own—a newborn grandmother
Am I, suckling light. . .
I am spiralling, I am spinning,
I am singing this Grandmother's Song.
I am remembering forever, where we
Belong.

—"SONG OF THE SELF: THE GRANDMOTHER"
BY ALMA LUZ VILLANUEVA

Shan Goshorn, Wolf-Clan Cherokee, created this handcolored black and white photograph "Honoring Full Moon" as part of her series, *Moontime: The Cycles of Life.* A Grandmother stands alone, surrounded by the white light of the full moon, creating another full moon in her hands. She represents the old wisewoman, creating light and life. The Grandmother, the Mother of the Mother, is the original creatrix, "the void, the womb of remembrance."

When we ignore the Grandmother, we lose one of our most precious resources. When we honor her, we benefit from the wisdom and knowledge of one who has walked so many years on the Earth, one through whom generations have gained life.

Old women, both mythical and human, continue to be revered in many parts of the world. In Wicca, the old religion of Europe, the Crone completes the Maiden and Mother as the Triple Goddess. In African societies, whether matrilineal or patrilineal, the counsel of the oldest woman is of great importance because she represents the mystery of women's power to give birth. The Native American Seneca say that Earth Island was built upon the back of Grandmother Turtle, who lives in the great Void of Space. Among the Kiowa, the sacred center of the community is the Ten Grandmother Bundles, containers for sacred objects. A Mayan prayer refers to "the grandmother of the sun, grandmother of the light."

According to Paula Gunn Allen, the Grandmothers are returning soon, and we want to be ready for them. Of all of us the Grandmother has the capacity to bring forth the best possible world, precisely because she is old, precisely because she draws on her knowledge of the ever-renewing cycles. Let us move again towards a time when we fortify ourselves with the counsel of the elders, particularly that of the Grandmothers. Let us turn to the source of life, that we may learn how to live. Let us listen to the ancient wisdom of the Sacred Feminine. Let us journey to our Grandmothers, our foremothers of spirit and of blood.

THE GODDESS IS ALIVE

OCHUMARE

NORTH AMERICA, CONTEMPORARY

Rainbow Woman, Rainbow Woman
Shining being, eternally wise
Dancing across the ancient skies.
Rainbow Woman, please come!
Rainbow Woman, bring your healing light to me.
Rainbow Woman, please come!
Restore the beauty within me.
—"RAINBOW WOMAN," A SONG BY LISA THIEL

Contemporary artist Asungi writes of her Rainbow Goddess Ochumare:

I believe that Ochumare's roots lie her-storically between the Dahomey peoples who worship the Rainbow Serpent as an aspect of Creatress Mawu and the Yoruba peoples who worship Ochun as Goddess of All Waters. Ochumare is the link between the Goddesses of the Universe and the Goddesses of the Earth. Here, She rests in the beauty of self-awareness. The Earth in Her lap is spinning from the cosmic energy that She provides from Her navel.

The Rainbow Goddess is revered through-out the world. In Greek mythology she is the Messenger Goddess Iris, for the rainbow is often seen as a link between heaven and earth. The Chibcha of South America also see the rainbow as a Goddess. To the Zulu, the rain-bow is the Queen's Arch, holding up the house of the Goddess of the Sky. The Lovedu, a Bantu tribe, were ruled for centuries by queens who held the secret of rainmaking. Despite colonialism, the contemporary queen, Mujaji IV,

maintains a powerful role as the Transformer of Clouds who can bring rain to her thirsty land.

The rainbow has long been regarded as a bridge traversed by the deities or as a way to journey between the realms. An old European tradition holds that anyone who passes under a rainbow will be transformed, from woman to man or man to woman. Ochumare, as a Rainbow Goddess of our era, offers us a similar great gift of transformation: the opportunity to evolve beyond the patriarchal divisions between heaven and earth, feminine and mascu-line, and among the races, sexes and classes.

She is a symbol of the peaceful co-existence and interdependence of all peoples. For we can work together and bring healing to the planet only if each of us is able to retain the integrity of her unique being. Ochumare unites the energies of all beings, creating the rainbow as a visual symbol of harmony and balance. We carry out her work, and that of all the Goddesses of the world, as we honor traditions that bring peace and balance to the planet. Co-existing and co-creating, we are a brilliant array, the rainbow bridge to a new world.

Become Ochumare.
Feel the Earth in your lap.
Take care of her.

CELEBRATION

GODDESS OF RAINBOWS · OL-U-MARE · ©PL ASUNGA

THE GODDESS IS ALIVE

We are creating a new world at this very moment.
At this very moment, we are traveling
the rainbow bridge.
The Yoruba people say that the rainbow is
the pride of heaven.

TEXT NOTES

GENERAL INTRODUCTION

In most parts of the world, the cooperative matrilineal and matrifocal (centered on the mother) group was gradually replaced by the more hierarchical patrifocal structure, eventually becoming patriarchy, or rule of the father. Many scholars believe that this hierarchy evolved with the surplus of goods created by agriculture, invented, ironically enough, by women, who obviously thought at the time that it was a good idea.

CREATION INTRODUCTION

Paula Gunn Allen writes in *The Sacred Hoop*, "Before the coming of the white man, or long ago, so far, as the people say, the Grandmother(s) created the firmament, the earth, and all the spirit beings in it. She (or they) created, by thinking into being, the Women, or the Woman, from whom the people sprang. The Women thus thought into being also gave thought, and the people and all the orders of being in this world came into being, including the laws, the sciences, agriculture, householding, social institutions—everything. Long ago the peoples of this hemisphere knew that their power to live came to them from the Grandmother or Grandmothers (depending on the tribe) not only originally but continuously, even to the present. Many old mythologies and most ceremonial cycles reiterate and celebrate this central fact of tribal Native American existence."

THE GREAT GODDESS OF LAUSSEL

Moontime is important, most obviously to women but to men as well, in predicting fertile psychic periods for ritual and meditation. Notations appear in Hindu Tantric art as guides to the lunar fluctuations of sensitivity in a woman's body, the worship of which is the focal point of Tantric ceremony. In fact, Sarasvati, the Hindu Goddess revered from Nepal to Bali, is said to have invented all the arts, including writing, numbers and mathematics.

SPIDER THE CREATRIX

The people of the island of Nauru in the South Pacific say that Old-Spider, Mother of All, who possessed the magic of the universe, created Earth and sky, moon, sun and Milky Way out of the darkness. For the Andaman Islanders in the Bay of Bengal, she is Biliku, the benign Ancestor who saves the people from eternal night by teaching them the magical arts of fire, song and dance.

AKUA'BA

Because we are all part of Mawu, fighting and aggression are self-destructive. This viewpoint is echoed in the Native American belief that we are all part of Spider Woman's web and in the Buddhist attitude that if we harm another being, even an insect, we harm a part of ourselves.

BREAST BOWL

Three is a number sacred to the Goddess around the world, as in the Celtic Triple Goddess, the phases of the moon and the three realms of existence (the underworld, Earth and heaven).

GUANYIN

Sickman and Soper state that "In general, all the Bodhisattvas are considered to be without gender, or, more strictly speaking, to combine the spiritual virtues of both sexes." Wai-kam Ho, curator of Chinese art at the Nelson-Atkins Museum, which houses this Guanyin, says that in popular thought since the 10–11th century c.e., Guanyin, who evolved from the Indian male Avalokiteshvara, is conceived of and accepted as female. Mr. Ho further states that the dress of an Indian prince shown here is the appropriate attire for all Bodhisattvas and that the Guanyin depicted here expresses the ideals of female beauty. Although there is some confusion over the sexual identity of early Guanyin images, Sickman and Soper, Ho and Dr. Patricia Berger all consider this Guanyin as female or tending towards the feminine.

ISIS LEADING NOFRETARI

Legend tells us that Isis ruled over Egypt, sending Osiris abroad to teach people her discoveries of agriculture and healing. Set, their cruel brother, murdered Osiris and scattered the fourteen pieces of his body, hoping to ensure the triumph of evil. Isis searched throughout her land, gathering the pieces. She performed the first embalming ritual, thus immortalizing Osiris. Changing herself into a bird, she hovered over his body and conceived Horus, the sun.

GRANDMOTHER GROWTH

Like the Kwakiutl Dzonokwa, Grandmother Growth wears a beard, perhaps because shamanism has come to be identified largely with men, although there are important Huichol women shamans. The beard might also symbolize the shaman's androgynous nature. In many parts of the world, lesbian and homosexual shamans are particularly revered because they embody a wide range of human experience and wisdom.

PERSEPHONE AND DEMETER

Persephone's Latin name, Proserpina, meaning "First Serpent," reflects her chthonic nature. According to classical writers, the tradition of Persephone and Demeter has its roots in the Minoan civilization of Crete and in the worship of Isis in Egypt. The spiritual and psychological power of the Eleusinian mysteries was so great that it was said, even by the patriarch Homer, "Happy are they among people upon Earth who have seen these mysteries."

YONI ROCKS

This quote from a Navajo menstruation ceremony describes the reverence for women's blood: *"A girl for whom it is the very first time. . .that the blood flows through her she tells about it: 'Blood has indeed flowed through me. Now it is all right!'. . .She at once comes to be called Menstruating for the First Time. All right! Now it is this way: at once she is decorated."*

APHRODITE

Protector of navigators, Aphrodite is often depicted with a dolphin, who shares her friendly and playful nature. To commemorate her seabirth, the women of ancient Cyprus ritualistically bathed a statue of the Goddess in the sea and then decorated it with flowers.

As the descendant of Ishtar and Inanna, Aphrodite is associated with Venus, the morning and evening star which bears her Roman name. Like Ochun she is associated with gold, for gold reflects light and never tarnishes.

THE APSARAS

Reflecting the biases of his gender and culture, a thirteenth century c.e. Chinese visitor described the Khmer women as "extremely lascivious," for they felt sexual soon after childbirth. He also reported that if a husband refused his wife, he was abandoned. If her partner was away for more than a few nights, a Khmer woman was likely to say "I am not a spirit! How can I sleep alone?"

GRANDMOTHER MOON

The following is my adaptation of a classic meditation honoring our connection with our foremothers created by Betsy Damon in 1974. It is available on my *Womanspirit Meditation Tape*, with music by Georgia Kelly: *Close your eyes and take a few deep breaths. Imagine that you go to a place in Nature that is special to you. Waiting there are older women who are important to you. They might be relatives, teachers, friends or spirit helpers. They reach out their hands to you and pick you up, cradling you in their arms. They begin to pass you back, hand over hand, generation through generation. You are passed back. . .back. . .back in time to a place that is a source of the Sacred Feminine. The women put you down gently. . .You look around and see the Grandmother, the Crone, the Wise One watching you. Go over to her and greet her: Ask her what you need to learn from her about bringing her wisdom back to the planet. . .Spend as long as you like with the Grandmother. When you are ready to leave, ask her to give you a symbol of her wisdom to take back with you. . .Thank her and return to the line of women. Feel them pick you up and pass you forward through time, their hands caressing you, passing you back to your special place. . .When you are ready, stretch and open your eyes. Write or draw the teachings and gift you received from the Grandmother, that you may remember daily to honor her in your life.*

REFERENCES

Key: The references for the opening quotes are in **Bold**. The works of authors of more than one book are numbered in the bibliography for easy reference.

Introduction
Campbell (4)
Evans, Linda
Fingland
Flanigan
Highwater (1)
Littlefeather
Loth
Noble
Razak
Sanchez
Sproul
Sutherland (1)

Creation Introduction
Allen, Max
Gimbutas
de Naie
Olson
Razak
Roos et al.
Sproul
Sutherland (1)

The Great Goddess of Willendorf
Boer
Campbell (4)
Johnson
Marshack
Noble (3)
Olson
Roos

The Great Goddess of Laussel
ARAS
Campbell (4)
Johnson
Marshack
Noble (3)
Reclaiming Community
Roos

The Bird-Headed Snake Goddess
Campbell (4)
Gimbutas (1)
Graves (1)
Iglehart, Harriet S.
Johnson
Neumann
Noble (3)
Sutherland (1)

Ixchel the Weaver
Furst and Furst
Johnson
Noble (3)
Sjöö and Mor
Turner
Williams, Anne

Spider the Creatrix
Allen, Paula Gunn (1)
Bahti
Campbell (4)
Cherry and McLeish
Johnson
Stone (1)
Todd
Tyler

Akua'ba
Adapted from **Cherry and McLeish**
Noble (3)
Schmalenbach
Sieber and Walker
Stone (1)
Walker, Roslyn Adele
Wassing

*All Mother and the
    Djanggawo Sisters*
Berndt (1) [Sisters]
Campbell (4) [Opening]
Cherry and McLeish [Sisters]
Johnson [All Mother]
Monaghan [All Mother and
    Sisters]
Noble (3) [All Mother]
Rothenberg [Closing]

Tlazolteotl
Furst and Furst (2)
Mariechild and Goodman (2)
Noble (1)
Rothenberg
Washbourn

The Birth Goddess of Catal Huyuk
Allen, Max
Allen, Paula Gunn (1)
Eisler
Johnson
Mellaart
Sjöö

Gwandusu
Banghart
Parrinder
Razak
Schmalenbach
Sieber and Walker
Walker, Roslyn Adele
Wassing

Breast Bowl
Burland
Castle
Emmerich
Johnson
Lehrman
Todd et al.

Diana of Ephesus
Banghart
Johnson
Noble (3)

The Woodlands Nursing Mother
Canan
Johnson
Naylor
Schmalenbach
Washbourn [prayer]

Amaterasu
Banghart
Cavendish
Colbert

Johnson
Kinsley (1)
Graves (2)
Stone (1)
Sutherland (2)

Mahuika
Banghart
Johnson
Kahukiwa and Grace
Noble (3)
Stone (1)

Nut
Gimbutas (1)
Ions
Neumann
Noble (3)
Rothenberg
Stone (2)

Queen Maya
Berger
Cutts
Johnson
Larson, Pal and Gowen
Noble (3)
Sutherland (2)
Zimmer

Hahai'i Wuhti
Bahti
Banghart
Dockstader
Lenz
Malotki and Lomatuway'ma
Museum of Northern Arizona
Washburn
Waters
Wright

Mary, Mother of God
Ashe (2)
Ehrenreich and English (2)
Larson, Pal and Gowen
Neumann
Warner, Marina

La Virgen de Guadalupe
Anzaldúa
Banghart
Galland
Kinsley (1)
Larson, Pal and Gowen

Mariechild and Goodman (2)
Turner

Guanyin
Berger
Blofeld (meditation)
Ho
Kinsley (1)
Leach and Fried
Sutherland (1)
Kato, et al.

Tara
ARAS
Sutherland (1 and 2)
Willson

Isis Leading Queen Nofretari
Ashe (3)
Apuleius
Asungi
Ions
Leach and Fried
Stone (1)

Ixchel and the Rabbit
Blodgett
Johnson
National Geographic Magazine
Noble (3)
Rasmussen (2)
Vogel

Artemis
Bolen
Johnson
Leach and Fried
Stone (1)

Shalako Mana
Allen, Paula Gunn (1)
Dockstader
Thiel (1)
Weigle

Goddess of the Sea
Banghart
Bullitt
Monaghan
Noble (1)
San Souci
Warner, Rex

Grandmother Growth
Allen, Paula Gunn (1)
Campbell (4)

Noble (3)
Rothenberg
Valadez
Williams

Transformation Introduction
Bahti
Gleason
Klaver
Mookerjee (3)
Murphy
Noble (1)
Roos
Starhawk (2)

Aditi
Monaghan
Mookerjee (3) and Sutherland (2)
Mookerjee and Khanna
Smithsonian Institution (2)
Vequaud

Pele
Banghart
Emerson
Kanahele
Kane
Razak
Stone (1)

The Motherpeace Death Card
Budapest
Campbell (4)
Noble (3)
Sjöö and Mor
Vogel and Noble

Persephone and Demeter
Banghart
Friedrich
Graves (1)
Johnson
Neumann
Perera
Spretnak (1)
Stone (1)

Inanna
Banghart
Barnstone
Kinsley (1)
Perera
Qualls-Corbett
Wolkstein and Kramer

Dzonokwa
Banghart
Brodzky, Danesewich and Johnson
Delzell
Jonaitis
LaChapelle
Levi-Strauss
Noble (3)

Kali Ma
Banghart
Chakravarty
Mookerjee (1)
Mookerjee and Khanna
Noble (3)

Nut, Mother of Rebirth
Neumann
Noble (3)
Rothenberg
Sutherland (1)

The Tomb Priestess
Bierhorst (1)
Murphy [song]
Noble (3)
Ragghianti

Hine-titama
Kahukiwa and Grace
Kane
Monaghan
Sutherland (1)

Coatlique
Anton
Anzaldúa
Furst and Furst
Johnson
Noble (3)
Washbourn

Selket
Banghart
Budge
Gilbert
Johnson
Monaghan
Neumann
Noble (3)
Sutherland (1)
Walker, Barbara G.

Gabon Ancestor Mask
Huet
Jahn

Sieber and Walker
Walker, Roslyn Adele (1)
Wassing

The Minoan Snake Priestess
Eisler
Hawkes
Johnson
Noble (4)

The Cycladic Goddess
Getz-Preziosi
Noble (3)

The Chanting Priestess
Banghart
Emmerich
Los Angeles County Museum of Art
Noble (3)
Plaskow and Christ
Rothenberg

The Oracular Goddess
Gimbutas (1)
Marshack
Noble (3)
Rawson (1)

Bird Woman
Banghart
Bierhorst (2)
Blodgett
Johnson
Noble (3)
Saward

The Gelede Mask
Drewal
Huet
Parrinder
Pericot-Garcia, Galloway and
    Lommel
Thompson
Walker, Roslyn Adele (2)
Wassing

The Dreaming Goddess
Castle
Coxhead and Hiller
Garfield
Noble (3)
Westwood

Celebration Introduction
Banghart
Berndt

Lorde
Mookerjee (1 and 2)
Mookerjee (3)
Sjöö and Mor
Sproul
Starhawk (2 and 3)
Teish and Amini
Wolkstein and Kramer

The Cosmic Yoni
ARAS
Mookerjee (2)
Rawson (1)

Yoni Rocks
Bahti
McGowan
LaChapelle
Littlefeather
Opler
Vogel
Washbourn [notes, quote and song]

Shakti
Mookerjee (2)
Noble (3)
Rawson (1)
Sjöö

Open Goddesses
Allen, Max
Anderson
    Adya-Shakti:
        Mookerjee (2)
    Heraldic Woman:
        Anderson
    Sheela-na-gig:
        Banghart
        Sharkey
        Sjöö
    Manubi:
        Berndt (1)
        Sproul
    Ancestor Spirit:
        Anderson
        Boltin and Newton
        Monaghan
        Pericot-Garcia, Galloway and
            Lommel
    The Doorway:
        Vogel and N'Diaye

Green Gulch Green Tara
Beyer
Oda
Sutherland
Thiel

R E F E R E N C E S

Vajravarahi
Allione
Noble (3)
Rawson (1 and 2)
Vogel
Wisdom Publications

The Goddess as Yogini
Mookerjee (1) [three quotes]
Mookerjee (3)
Sutherland (1)

Lilith
Banghart
Johnson
Koltuv
Monaghan
Noble (3)

Ishtar
Banghart
Stone (1)
Walker, Barbara G.

Aphrodite
Barnard [poem]
Bolen (1)

Bradley (1)
Brinkerhoff
Friedrich
Kinsley (1)

Xochiquetzal
Anton
Burland
Campbell (4)
Furst and Furst
Johnson
Mookerjee (1)
Noble (3)
Rothenberg
Stone (1)

The Apsaras
Leach and Fried
Monaghan
Noble (3)
Swann

The Horned Goddess
Campbell (4)
Conrad-Da'oud
Lhote
Noble (3)

Ochun
Asungi
Olson
Teish

Gaia's Children
Seed, Macy, Fleming, Naess

Kannon with Sword
Banghart
Blofeld
Kinsley (1)
Noble (3)
Oda
Schaef (1)
Sutherland (1)

Grandmother Moon
Allen, Paula Gunn (1)
Canan
Damon
Villanueva
Walker, Roslyn Adele (1)

Ochumare
Asungi
Parrinder
Thiel (1)

Adair, Margo. *Working Inside Out.* Berkeley, CA: Wingbow Press, 1984.

Allen, Max. *The Birth Symbol in Traditional Women's Art, From Eurasia and the Western Pacific.* Toronto: The Museum for Textiles, 1981.

*Allen, Paula Gunn (1). *The Sacred Hoop: Recovering the Feminine in American Indian Traditions.* Boston: Beacon Press, 1986.

--- (2). *Spider Woman's Granddaughters.* Boston: Beacon Press, 1989.

*Allione, Tsultrim. *Women of Wisdom.* London: Routledge & Kegan Paul, 1984.

Anderson, Richard L. *Art in Primitive Societies.* Englewood Cliffs, NJ: Prentice-Hall, 1979.

Anton, Ferdinand. *Woman in Pre-Columbian America.* New York: Abner Schram, 1973.

Anzaldúa, Gloria. "Entering into the Serpent." In Plaskow and Christ, eds., *Weaving the Visions: New Patterns in Feminist Spirituality.* San Francisco: Harper & Row, 1989.

Apuleius. *The Golden Ass.* Robert Graves, trans. New York: Farrar, Straus & Giroux, 1977.

ARAS (The Archive for Research in Archetypal Symbolism), San Francisco, 1989.

Arguelles, Miriam and José Arguelles. *The Feminine: Spacious as the Sky.* Boulder, CO: Shambhala, 1977.

Ashe, Geoffrey (1). *The Glastonbury Tor Maze.* Somerset, England: At the Foot of the Tree Publishers, 1979.

--- (2). Private Interview, Glastonbury, U.K., 1980.

--- (3). *The Virgin.* London: Routledge & Kegan Paul, 1976.

Aston, W.G., trans. *Nihongi.* Rutland, VT and Kyoto, Japan: Charles E. Tuttle Co., 1972.

Asungi. Personal Interviews. Los Angeles, 1988–89.

Bachofen, J.J. *Myth, Religion, & Mother Right.* Princeton, NJ: Princeton University Press, 1967.

Bahti, Tom. *Southwestern Indian Ceremonies.* Las Vegas, NV: KC Publications, 1970, 1987.

Banghart, Gina. Personal Interview. Pt. Reyes, CA, 1989.

Barnard, Mary, trans. *Sappho: A New Translation.* Berkeley: University of California Press, 1958.

Barnstone, Willis and Aliki Barnstone, eds. *Book of Women Poets from Antiquity to Now.* New York: Schocken Books, 1980.

Begg, Ean. *The Cult of the Black Virgin.* London and New York: Routledge & Kegan Paul, 1985.

Berger, Pamela. *The Goddess Obscured: Transformation of the Grain Protectress from Goddess to Saint.* Boston: Beacon Press, 1985.

Berger, Patricia, Dr., Curator of Chinese Art, Asian Art Museum, San Francisco. Telephone interview, 1990.

Berndt, Ronald M., ed. (1). *Australian Aboriginal Art.* New York and London: The Macmillan Company and Collier-Macmillan, 1964.

--- (2). *Love Songs of Arnhem Land.* Chicago: University of Chicago Press, 1976.

Berndt, Ronald M. and Katherine M. Berndt. *Man, Land and Myth in North Australia.* East Lansing, MI: Michigan State University Press, 1970.

Beyer, Stephan. *The Cult of Tara.* Berkeley: The University of California Press, 1978.

Bierhorst, John, ed. (1). *In the Trail of the Wind: American Indian Poems and Ritual Orations.* New York: Farrar, Straus and Giroux, 1972.

--- (2). *The Sacred Path: Spells, Prayers & Power Songs of the American Indians.* New York: Quill, 1984.

Blodgett, Jean. *The Coming & Going of the Shaman: Eskimo Shamanism and Art.* Winnipeg: Winnipeg Art Gallery, 1978.

Blofeld, John. *Bodhisattva of Compassion: The Mystical Tradition of Kuan Yin.* Boulder, CO: Shambhala, 1978.

Body Mind Spirit, Editors of. *The New Age Catalog.* New York: Dolphin Books, Doubleday, 1988.

Boer, Charles. *The Homeric Hymns.* Chicago: Swallow Press, 1970.

Bolen, Jean Shinoda (1). *Goddesses in Every Woman: A New Psychology of Women.* San Francisco: Harper & Row, 1984.

--- (2). *The Tao of Psychology: Synchronicity and the Self.* San Francisco: Harper & Row, 1982.

Boltin, Lee, and Douglas Newton. *Masterpieces of Primitive Art.* New York: Alfred A. Knopf, 1978.

Boucher, Sandy. *Turning the Wheel: American Women Creating the New Buddhism.* San Francisco: Harper & Row, 1988.

Bradley, Marion Zimmer (1). *The Firebrand.* New York: Simon & Schuster, 1987.

--- (2). *The Mists of Avalon.* New York: Ballantine Books, 1982.

Bramly, Serge. *Macumba: The Teachings of Maria-Jose, Mother of the Gods.* New York: St. Martin's Press, 1975.

Briffault, Robert. *The Mothers.* London: George Allen & Unwin Ltd., 1959.

Brinkerhoff, Dericksen Morgan. *Hellenistic Statues of Aphrodite.* New York and London: Garland Publishing, Inc., 1978.

Brodzky, Anne Trueblood, Rose Daneswich and Nick Johnson, eds. *Stones, Bones and Skin: Ritual and*

*general background
**recommended for children

Shamanic Art. Toronto: The Society for Art Publications, 1977.

Brooks, Charles V.W. *Sensory Awareness: The Rediscovery of Experiencing.* New York: The Viking Press, 1974.

Brose, David S., James A. Brown and David W. Penney. *Ancient Art of the American Woodland Indians.* New York: Harry N. Abrams, Inc. in association with the Detroit Institute of Arts, 1985.

Brown, Lester R., William U. Chandler, Alan Durning and Christopher Flavin. *State of the World.* New York: W.W. Norton, 1988.

Bryant, Dorothy. *The Kin of Ata Are Waiting for You.* Berkeley/New York: Moon Books/Random House, 1976.

Budge, E.A. Wallis. *The Book of the Dead.* Secaucus, NJ: University Books, Inc., 1960.

Buehler, Alfred, Terry Barrow and Charles P. Montford. *The Art of the South Sea Islands.* New York: Crown Publishing, 1962.

Bullitt, Patricia. Telephone Interview, 1989.

Bunch, Charlotte, ed. *Quest: A Feminist Quarterly:* "Women and Spirituality". Vol. 1, no. 4, Spring, 1975.

Burland, Cottie. *North American Indian Mythology.* London: Paul Hamlyn, 1965, 1975.

Cagnon, Denise, and Gail Groves, eds. *Her Wits About Her: Self Defense Success Stories by Women.* New York: Harper & Row, 1987.

Cameron, Anne. *Daughters of Copper Woman.* Vancouver, BC: Press Gang Publishers, 1981.

Cameron, D.O. *Symbols of Birth and Death in the Neolithic Era.* London: Kenyon-Deane, 1981.

Campbell, Joseph (1). *Historical Atlas of World Mythology: The Way of the Seeded Earth, Part 1, The Sacrifice.* New York: Harper & Row, 1988.

--- (2). *The Masks of God: Primitive Mythology.* New York: Penguin Books, 1976.

--- (3). *The Mythic Image.* Princeton, NJ: Princeton University Press, 1974.

--- (4). *The Way of the Animal Powers,* vol. 1. London: Alfred van der Marck, 1983.

Canan, Janine, ed. *She Rises Like the Sun.* Freedom, CA: The Crossing Press, 1989.

Carson, Anne, ed. *Feminist Spirituality & the Feminine Divine: An Annotated Bibliography.* Trumansburg, NY: The Crossing Press, 1986.

Castle, Leila and Christopher Castle. Personal Interview. Pt. Reyes, CA, 1989.

Cavendish, Richard, ed. *An Illustrated Encyclopedia of Mythology.* New York: Crescent Books, 1984.

Chakravarty, Shuma, interviewed by Kathleen Alexander-Berghorn. "The Dark Devi." *Woman of Power,* Winter, issue 8, 1988.

Cheatham, Annie, and Mary Clare Powell. *This Way Daybreak Comes.* Philadelphia: New Society Publishers, 1986.

**Cherry, Helen and Kenneth McLeish. *In the Beginning: Creation Myths from Around the World.* Essex, England: Longman House, 1984.

Chicago, Judy. *The Dinner Party.* Garden City, NY: Anchor Books, 1979.

Chicago, Judy, with Susan Hill. *Embroidering Our Heritage: The Dinner Party Needlework.* Garden City, NY: Anchor Books, 1980.

Christ, Carol P. (1). *Diving Deep and Surfacing: Women Writers On A Spiritual Quest.* Boston: Beacon Press, 1980.

--- (2). *Laughter of Aphrodite.* San Francisco: Harper & Row, 1987.

Christ, Carol P., and Judith Plaskow, eds. *Womanspirit Rising: A Feminist Reader in Religion.* San Francisco: Harper & Row, 1979.

Coe, Michael, Dean Snow and Elizabeth Benson. *Atlas of Ancient America.* New York: Facts on File, Inc., 1986.

Coe, Ralph T., exhibition organizer. *Sacred Circles: Two Thousand Years of North American Indian Art.* Kansas City, MO: Nelson Gallery of Art—Atkins Museum of Fine Arts, 1977.

Collins, Sheila D. *A Different Heaven and Earth.* Valley Forge, PA: Judson Press, 1974.

Colton, Harold S. *Hopi Kachina Dolls.* Albuquerque: University of New Mexico Press, 1949, 1959, 1973.

Conrad-Da'oud, Emilie, interviewed by Carolyn Schaffer. *Yoga Journal,* issue 77, November/December 1987.

Conze, Edward. *Buddhist Studies.* San Francisco: Wheelwright Press, Zen Center, 1967.

Cory, Kate. *The Hopi Photographs.* Albuquerque: University of New Mexico Press, 1986.

Coxhead, David and Susan Hiller. *Dreams: Visions of the Night.* New York: Avon Books, 1975.

Cutts, Linda. Personal Interview. Zen Center, San Francisco, 1988.

Daly, Mary. *Beyond God the Father: Toward a Philosophy of Women's Liberation.* Boston: Beacon Press, 1973.

Dames, Michael. *The Silbury Treasure: The Great Goddess Rediscovered.* London: Thames and Hudson, 1976.

Damon, Betsy. Workshop given in San Francisco, 1981.

de Naie, Lucienne. Personal Interview. Huelo, HI, October, 1988.

Delzell, Donna. Jesse Peter Memorial Museum. Personal Interview. Santa Rosa, CA, 1988.

Demetrakopoulos, Stephanie. *Listening to Our Bodies: The Rebirth of Feminine Wisdom.* Boston: Beacon Press, 1983.

Diner, Helen. *Mothers and Amazons: The First Feminine History of Culture.* Garden City, NY: Anchor Press, 1973.

Dockstader, Frederick J. *The Kachina & the White Man: The Influence of White Culture on the Hopi Kachina.* Albuquerque: University of New Mexico Press, 1954, 1985.

Downing, Christine. *The Goddess: Mythical Images of the Feminine.* New York: Crossroad, 1987.

Drewal, Henry. Personal Communication. Cleveland State University, 1989.

Duane, Diane. *The Door Into Shadow.* New York: Bluejay Books, Inc., 1983.

**Dutton, Bertha, and Caroline Olin. *Myths & Legends of Indians of the Southwest.* Santa Barbara, CA: Bellerophon Books, 1985.

Eaton, Evelyn. *I Send a Voice.* Wheaton, IL: Theosophical Publishing House, 1978.

Edelson, Mary Beth. *Seven Cycles: Public Rituals.* New York: Mary Beth Edelson, 1980.

Ehrenreich, Barbara, and Dierdre English (1). *Complaints and Disorders: The Sexual Politics of Sickness.* Old Westbury, NY: The Feminist Press, 1973.

--- (2). *Witches, Midwives and Nurses.* Old Westbury, NY: The Feminist Press, 1973.

*Eisler, Riane. *The Chalice & the Blade: Our History, Our Future.* San Francisco: Harper & Row, 1987.

Emerson, A.M., M.D. *Pele and Hiiaka—A Myth from Hawaii.* Rutland, VT and Tokyo: Charles E. Tuttle Co., Inc., 1915, 1978.

Emmerich, Andre. *Art Before Columbus: The Art of Ancient Mexico from the Archaic Villages of the Second Millennium.* New York: Simon & Schuster, 1963.

Erdoes, Richard, and Alfonso Ortiz, eds. *American Indian Myths and Legends.* New York: Pantheon Books, 1984.

Evans, Arthur. *Witchcraft and the Gay Counterculture.* Boston: Fag Rag Books, 1978.

Evans, Linda. Personal Communication, 1989.

Evelyn-White, Hugh G., trans. *Hesiod, the Homeric Hymns.* London and Cambridge, MA: Loeb Classical Library, 1920.

Ezra, Kate. *A Human Ideal in African Art: Bamana Figurative Sculpture.* Washington, DC: Smithsonian Institution Press for the National Museum of African Art, 1986.

Fagg, William. *Yoruba Sculpture of West Africa.* New York: Alfred A. Knopf, 1982.

Falk, Nancy A., and Rita M. Gross, eds. *Unspoken Words.* San Francisco: Harper & Row, 1980.

Feder, Norman. *Two Hundred Years of North American Indian Culture.* New York: Praeger Publishing in association with the Whitney Museum of American Art, 1971.

Fingland, Randy. Editorial Communication, Berkeley, 1989.

Fitzhugh, William W., and Susan A. Kaplan. *Inua.* Washington, DC: Smithsonian Institution Press, 1982.

Flanigan, Michael. Personal Interview. ARAS, Jung Institute of San Francisco, 1989.

Fortune, Dion. *The Sea Priestess.* New York: Samuel Weiser, 1978.

Friedrich, Paul. *The Meaning of Aphrodite.* Chicago: University of Chicago Press, 1978.

Fundaburk, Emma Lila, and Mary Douglass Foreman, eds. *Sun Circles and Human Hands: The Southeastern Indians Art and Industries.* Luverne, AL: Emma Lila Fundaburk, 1957.

Furst, Peter T. and Jill L. Furst. (1). *North American Indian Art.* New York: Rizzoli Int., 1984.

--- (2). *Pre-Columbian Art of Mexico.* New York: Abbeville Press, 1980.

Galland, China (1). Public lecture: "Tara and the Black Madonna." Zen Center, San Francisco, 1988.

--- (2). *Women in the Wilderness.* New York: Harper & Row, 1980.

Gardner, Helen, ed. *The New Oxford Book of English Verse.* Oxford: Oxford University Press, 1972.

Garfield, Patricia L., Ph.D. *Creative Dreaming.* New York: Simon & Schuster, 1974.

Gearhart, Sally Miller. *The Wanderground: Stories of the Hill Women.* Watertown, MA: Persephone Press, 1978.

Geertz, Armin W., and Michael Lomatuway'ma. *Children of Cottonwood: Piety and Ceremonialism in Hopi Indian Puppetry.* Lincoln, NB and London: University of Nebraska Press, 1987.

Getz-Preziosi, Pat. *Early Cycladic Art in North American Collections.* Richmond, VA, Seattle and London: Virginia Museum of Fine Arts (Distributed by the University of Washington Press), 1987.

Gidlow, Elsa. *Elsa: I Come With My Songs.* San Francisco: Druid Heights Books/Bootlegger Press, 1986.

Gil, Eliana, Ph.D. *Outgrowing the Pain: A Book for and about Adults Abused as Children.* Walnut Creek, CA: Launch Press, 1983.

Gilbert, Katherine S., with Joan Holt and Sara Hudson, eds. *Treasures of Tutankhamun.* New York: The Metropolitan Museum of Art, 1976.

*Gimbutas, Marija (1). *The Goddesses and Gods of Old Europe.* Berkeley: University of California Press, 1982.

* --- (2). *The Language of the Goddess.* San Francisco: Harper & Row, 1989.

Gleason, Judith. *Oya, In Praise of the Goddess.* Boston and London: Shambhala Publications, 1987.

Goldenberg, Naomi R. *Changing of the Gods: Feminism & the End of Traditional Religions.* Boston: Beacon Press, 1979.

Govinda, Lama Anagarinka. *The Way of the White Clouds: A Buddhist Pilgrim in Tibet.* Berkeley: Shambhala, 1971.

Grahn, Judy. *Another Mother Tongue: Gay Words, Gay Worlds.* Boston: Beacon Press, 1984.

Graves, Robert (1). *The Greek Myths,* vol. 1. New York: Penguin Books, 1979.

--- (2). Introduction to *New Larousse Encyclopedia of Mythology.* New York: Prometheus Press, 1968.

Great Goddess Collective. *The Great Goddess.* New York: Heresies, A Feminist Publication on Art & Politics, 1982.

Greenwood, Sadja, M.D. *Menopause Naturally*. San Francisco: Volcano Press, 1984.

Griffin, Susan. *Woman and Nature: The Roaring Inside Her*. New York: Harper & Row, 1979.

Grigson, Geoffrey. *The Goddess of Love: The Birth, Death and Return of Aphrodite*. London: Constable & Co., 1976.

Grimal, Pierre, ed. *Larousse World Mythology*. Secaucus, NJ: Chartwell Books, Inc., 1965.

Hall, Nor (1). *The Moon and the Virgin*. New York: Harper & Row, 1980.

--- (2). *Mothers and Daughters*. Minneapolis: Rusoff Books, 1976.

Harrer, Heinrich. *Seven Years in Tibet*. Richard Graves, trans. London: Pan Books, Ltd., 1953.

Hawkes, Jacquetta. *Dawn of the Gods*. New York: Random House, 1968.

**Hawthorne, Terri Berthiaume, and Diane Berthiaume Brown. *Many Faces of the Great Mother: A Goddess Coloring Book for All Ages*. St. Paul, MN: Tara Educational Services, 1987.

Heilbrun, Carolyn B. *Toward a Recognition of Androgyny*. New York: Alfred A. Knopf, 1973.

Highwater, Jamake (1). *The Primal Mind: Vision and Reality in Indian America*. New York and Scarborough, Ontario: Meridian, 1981.

--- (2). *Ritual of the Wind: North American Indian Ceremonies, Music & Dance*. New York: Alfred Van Der Marck Editions, 1984.

Ho, Wai-kam, Laurence Sickman Curator of Chinese Art, Nelson-Atkins Museum, Kansas City, Missouri. Telephone Interview, 1990.

Hock, Nancy, Curator of Southeast Asian Art, Asian Art Museum of San Francisco. Private communication, 1990.

Homer. *The Iliad*. Richard Lattimore, trans. Chicago: University of Chicago Press, 1951.

Huet, Michael. *The Dance, Art & Ritual of Africa*. London: William Collins Sons & Co., Ltd., 1978.

Humphreys, Christmas. *A Popular Dictionary of Buddhism*. London: Curzon Press, 1984.

Huxley, Laura Archera. *You Are Not the Target*. No. Hollywood, CA: Wilshire Book Co., 1974.

Huyghe, Rene, ed. *Larousse Encyclopedia of Prehistoric and Ancient Art*. New York: Prometheus Press, 1962.

Iglehart, Harriet Austen Stokes. "The Feminine Image In the Mythology of Greece," unpublished, 1976.

*Iglehart, Hallie Austen. *Womanspirit: A Guide to Women's Wisdom*. San Francisco: Harper & Row, 1983.

*Iglehart, Hallie Austen. *Womanspirit Meditation Tape*. With music by Georgia Kelly. W.I.S.E., P.O. Box 697, Pt. Reyes, CA 94956. 1984.

Ions, Veronica. *Egyptian Mythology*. New York: Peter Bedrick Books, 1988.

Isaacs-Ashford, Janet. *Mothers & Midwives: A History of Traditional Childbirth*. Solano Beach, CA: Janet Isaacs-Ashford, 1988.

Jahn, Janheinz. *Muntu: An Outline of the New African Culture*. Marjorie Green, trans. New York: Grove Press, 1961.

Johari, Harish. *Tools for Tantra*. Rochester, VT: Inner Traditions International, Ltd., 1986.

Johnson, Buffie. *Lady of the Beasts: Ancient Images of the Goddess and Her Sacred Animals*. San Francisco: Harper & Row, 1988.

Jonaitis, Aldona. *From the Land of the Totem Poles: The Northwest Coast Indian Art Collection at the Museum of Natural History*. New York and Seattle: American Museum of Natural History and University of Washington Press, 1988.

Jordan, Wendy Adler. *By the Light of the Quilliq: Eskimo Life in the Canadian Arctic*. Washington, DC: Smithsonian Institution Press, 1979.

Jung, Carl. *Man and His Symbols*. London: Aldus Books Ltd., 1964.

Kahukiwa, Robyn, and Patricia Grace. *Wahine Toa: Women of Maori Myth*. Auckland: William Collins Publishers, Ltd., 1984.

Kanahele, Pualani. Personal Interview. Kahalui, HI, 1988.

Kane, Herb Kawainui. *Pele—Goddess of Hawaii's Volcanoes*. Captain Cook, HI: The Kawainui Press, 1987.

Kato, Bunno, Yoshiro Tamura and Kojiro Miyasaka, trans. *The Threefold Lotus Sutra*. New York and Tokyo: Weatherhill/Kosei, 1975.

Kelly, Mary B. "Goddess Embroideries of Russia and the Ukraine." *Woman's Art Journal*, vol. 4, no. 2, Fall 1983/Winter 1984.

Kent, Mary. *In the Shadow of a Goddess: A Healing Journey at Machu Picchu, Peru*. Kentfield, CA: Let Us Keep in Touch, 1981.

King, Sallie B., trans. and annotat. *Passionate Journey: The Spiritual Autobiography of Satomi Myodo*. Boston: Shambhala, 1987.

Kinsley, David (1). *The Goddesses' Mirror: Visions of the Divine from East and West*. Albany: State Universities of New York Press, 1989.

--- (2). *Hindu Goddesses: Visions of the Divine Feminine in the Hindu Religious Tradition*. Berkeley: University of California Press, 1986.

Koltuv, Barbara Black, Ph.D. *The Book of Lilith*. York Beach, ME: Nicolas-Hayes, Inc., 1986.

LaChapelle, Dolores. *Earth Wisdom*. Los Angeles, CA: The Guild of Tutors Press, 1978.

Lady Unique Collective. *Lady-Unique-Inclination-of-the-Night*. New Brunswick, NJ: Sowing Circle Press, 1976.

Lafaye, Jacques. *Quetzalcoatl and Guadalupe: The Formation of Mexican National Consciousness, 1531–1813*. Chicago: University of Chicago Press, 1976.

Lange, Kurt, and Max Hirmer. *Egypt: Architecture, Sculpture and Painting in 3000 Years*. London and New York: Phaidon Books, 1968.

Larson, Gerald James, Pratapaditya Pal and Rebecca P. Gowen. *In Her Image: The Great Goddess in Indian Asia and The Madonna in Christian Culture*. Santa Barbara: University of California at Santa Barbara Art Museum, University of California, 1980.

Leach, Maria, ed., and Jerome Fried, assoc. ed. *Funk & Wagnalls Standard Dictionary of Folklore, Mythology and Legend*. San Francisco: Harper & Row, 1984.

Le Guin, Ursula K. *Always Coming Home*. New York: Harper & Row, 1985.

Lehrman, Frederic. *The Sacred Landscape*. Berkeley, CA: Celestial Arts, 1988.

Lenz, Mary Jane. *The Stuff of Dreams: Native American Dolls*. New York: Museum of the American Indian, 1986.

Leonard, Jonathan Norton. *Ancient America*. New York: Time Life Books, Time Inc., 1967.

Levi-Strauss, Claude. *The Way of the Mask*. Sylvia Modelski, trans. Seattle: University of Washington Press, 1982.

Levine, Stephen. *Who Dies? An Investigation of Conscious Living and Conscious Dying*. Garden City, NY: Anchor Books, 1982.

Lhote, Henri. *The Search for the Tassili Frescoes*. New York: E.P. Dutton, 1959.

Lippard, Lucy R. *Overlay: Contemporary Art and the Art of Prehistory*. New York: Pantheon Books, 1983.

Littlefeather, Sacheen (Cruz). Personal Interview. San Anselmo, CA, 1989.

"The Living Maya." *National Geographic Magazine*. Vol. 148, no. 6, Dec., 1973.

Lorde, Audre. *Sister Outsider*. Trumansburg, NY: The Crossing Press, 1984.

Los Angeles County Museum of Art. *Masterworks of Mexican Art*. Los Angeles: Los Angeles County Museum of Art.

*Loth, Heinrich. *Woman in Ancient Africa*. Sheila Marnie, trans. Westport, CT: Lawrence Hill & Co., 1987.

Malotki, Ekkehart, and Michael Lomatuway'ma. *Earth Fire: A Hopi Legend of the Sunset Crater Eruption*. Flagstaff, AZ: Northland Press, 1987.

Mariechild, Diane (1). *Crystal Visions*. Trumansburg, NY: The Crossing Press, 1985.

––– (2). *Mother Wit: A Feminist Guide to Psychic Development*. Trumansburg, NY: The Crossing Press, 1981.

Mariechild, Diane, with Shuli Goodman (1). *The Inner Dance: A Guide to Spiritual & Psychological Unfolding*. Freedom, CA: The Crossing Press, 1987.

––– (2). Personal Interview. Pt. Reyes, CA, 1989.

Markale, Jean. *Women of the Celts*. London: Gordon Cremonesi Publishers, 1975.

Marshack, Alexander. *The Roots of Civilization*. New York: McGraw-Hill, 1972.

Matz, Friedrich. *The Art of Crete and Early Greece*. New York: Crown Publishers, 1962.

McGowan, Charlotte. *Ceremonial Fertility Sites in Southern California*. San Diego Museum Papers, no. 14. San Diego, CA: San Diego Museum of Man, 1982.

McKee, Char, ed. *Woman of Power: A Magazine of Feminism, Spirituality and Politics*. All issues.

Mellaart, James. *Earliest Civilizations of the Near East*. New York: McGraw-Hill Book Co., 1965.

Merry, Eleanor C. *The Year and Its Festivals*. London: Anthroposophical Publishing Co., 1952.

Metropolitan Museum of Art. *Art of Oceania, Africa & the Americas—From the Museum of Primitive Art*. New York: Metropolitan Museum of Art, 1969.

Monaghan, Patricia. *The Book of Goddesses and Heroines*. New York: E.P. Dutton, 1981. Reissued Llewellyn Press, 1990.

*Mookerjee, Ajit (1). *Kali: The Feminine Force*. New York: Destiny Books, 1988.

––– (2). *Tantra Art: Its Philosophy & Physics*. Basel, Paris, New Delhi: Ravi Kumar, 1983.

––– (3). *Tantra Asana: A Way to Self-Realization*. Basel, Paris, New Delhi: Ravi Kumar, 1971.

Mookerjee, Ajit, and Madhu Khanna. *The Tantric Way: Art, Science & Ritual*. Boston: New York Graphic Society/Little, Brown and Co., 1977.

Moon, Sheila. *Changing Woman and Her Sisters*. San Francisco: Guild for Psychological Studies, 1984.

Museum of Northern Arizona. *An Introduction to Hopi Kachina*. Flagstaff, AZ: Museum of Northern Arizona, 1977.

"Navaho Medicine." *Human Nature*. July, 1978.

Naylor, Maria, ed. *Authentic Indian Designs*. New York: Dover Publishing, 1975.

Neumann, Erich. *The Great Mother: An Analysis of the Archetype*. Ralph Manheim, trans. Princeton, NJ: Princeton University Press, 1955.

Noble, Vicki (1). "Female Blood Roots of Shamanism." *Shaman's Drum*, No. 4, Spring, 1986.

––– (2). *Motherpeace: A Way to the Goddess through Myth, Art and Tarot*. San Francisco: Harper & Row, 1983.

––– (3). Private Interview. Berkeley, CA, 1989.

––– (4), publisher/editor. *Snake Power: A Journal of Contemporary Female Shamanism*, 5856 College Ave., Box 138, Oakland, CA 94618.

Oda, Mayumi. *Goddesses*. Volcano, CA: Volcano Press, 1981.

Olson, Carl, ed. *The Book of the Goddess Past and Present*. New York: Crossroad, 1987.

BIBLIOGRAPHY

Opler, Morris E. *An Apache Life-way: The Economic, Social and Religious Institutions of the Chiricahua Indians.* Chicago: Univesity of Chicago Press, 1941.

Pagels, Elaine. *Adam, Eve and the Serpent.* New York: Random House, 1988.

Pal, Pratapaditya. *Indian Sculpture,* vol. 1. Berkeley, Los Angeles and London: Los Angeles County Museum, University of California Press, 1986.

Parrinder, Geoffrey. *African Mythology.* New York: Peter Bedrick Books, 1986.

Pepper, Elizabeth, and John Wilcock. *Magical & Mystical Sites.* New York: Harper & Row, 1977.

Perera, Sylvia Brinton. *Descent to the Goddess: A Way of Initiation for Women.* Toronto: Inner City Books, 1981.

Pericot-Garcia, Luis, John Galloway and Andreas Lommel. *Prehistoric & Primitive Art.* New York: Harry Abrams, 1967.

**Phelps, Ethel Johnston. *The Maid of the North: Feminist Folktales from Around the World.* New York: Holt, Rinehart & Winston, 1981.

Piankoff, Alexandre. *The Shrines of Tut-Ankh-Amon.* New York: Pantheon Books, 1955.

Plaskow, Judith, and Carol P. Christ, eds. *Weaving the Visions: New Patterns in Feminist Spirituality.* San Francisco: Harper & Row, 1989.

Platon, Nicholas. *Zakros: The Discovery of a Lost Palace of Ancient Crete.* New York: Charles Scribner's Sons, 1971.

Purce, Jill. *The Mystic Spiral: Journey of the Soul.* New York: Avon Books, 1974.

Qoyawayma, Polingaysi (Elizabeth Q. White). *No Turning Back: A Hopi Indian Woman's Struggle to Live in Two Worlds.* Albuquerque: University of New Mexico Press, 1964.

Qualls-Corbett, Nancy. *The Sacred Prostitute: Eternal Aspect of the Feminine.* Toronto: Inner City Books, 1988.

Ragghianti, C.L., ed. *National Museum of Anthropology, Mexico City.* New York: Newsweek, Inc., 1981.

Rasmussen, Knud (1). *Intellectual Culture of the Iglulik Eskimos: Report of the Fifth Thule Expedition 1921–24.* W.E. Calvert, trans. Copenhagen: Gyldendalske Boghandel, Nordisk Forlag, 1929.

––– (2). *Netsilik Eskimos: The Social Life and Spiritual Culture.* Copenhagen: Gyldendalske Boghandel, Nordisk Forlag, 1930.

Rawson, Phillip (1). *The Art of Tantra.* Greenwich, CT: New York Graphic Society, Ltd., 1973.

––– (2). *Tantra: The Indian Cult of Ecstasy.* New York: Bounty Books, 1973.

––– (3). Introduction to *Tantra,* a catalogue for the Hayward Gallery, London. London: Arts Council of Great Britain, 1971.

Razak, Arisika. Personal Interviews. Oakland, CA, 1988–89.

Redgrove, Peter. *The Black Goddess.* New York: Grove Press, 1987.

Ricc, Edward. *Eastern Definitions.* Garden City, NY: Anchor Books, 1980.

Richter, Gisela M. *A Handbook of Greek Art.* London: The Phaidon Press, 1959.

Roos, Sandra, Sally Gearhart, Chellis Glendinning, Hallie Iglehart and Yani Novak. *Chains of Fires: A Rediscovery of Womanspirit.* Unpublished manuscript, 1976.

Rothenberg, Jerome, ed. *Technicians of the Sacred.* Berkeley: University of California Press, 1985.

Ruether, Rosemary Radford. *Womanguides: Readings Toward a Feminist Theology.* Boston: Beacon Press, 1985.

Rush, Anne Kent. *Moon, Moon.* New York and Berkeley: Random House and Moon Books, 1976.

Russell, Letty M., Kwok Pui-lan, Ada Maria Isasi-Diaz and Katie Geneva Cannon, eds. *Inheriting our Mother's Gardens: Feminist Theology in Third World Perspective.* Philadelphia: The Westminster Press, 1988.

**San Souci, Robert D. *Song of Sedna.* New York: Doubleday, 1981.

Sanchez, Carol Lee. "New World Tribal Communities." In Plaskow and Christ, eds., *Weaving the Visions: New Patterns in Feminist Spirituality.* San Francisco: Harper & Row, 1989.

Sannella, Lee, M.D. *Kundalini—Psychosis or Transcendence?* San Francisco: H.S. Dakin Co., 1976.

Saunders, E. Dale. *Mudra: A Study of Symbolic Gestures in Japanese Buddhist Sculpture.* Princeton, NJ: Princeton University Press, 1960.

Saward, Jeff. *The Caerdroia Field Guide.* Essex, England: Caerdroia, 1987.

Schaef, Anne Wilson (1). *Co-Dependence: Misunderstood, Mistreated.* San Francisco: Harper & Row, 1986.

––– (2). *Women's Reality.* Minneapolis: Winston Press, Inc., 1981.

Schmalenbach, Werner, ed. *African Art, from the Barbier-Mueller Collection, Geneva.* Munich: Prestel-Verlag, 1988.

Seed, John, Joanna Macy, Pat Fleming and Arne Naess. *Thinking Like a Mountain: Toward A Council of All Beings.* Philadelphia and Santa Cruz, CA: New Society Publishers, 1988.

Shaman's Drum: A Journal of Experiential Shamanism. Berkeley, CA. All issues.

Shao, Paul. *Asiatic Influences in Pre-Columbian American Art.* Ames, IA: Iowa State University Press, 1976.

Sharkey, John. *Celtic Mysteries.* New York: Crossroad, no. 6, Church of St. Mary & St. David, 1975.

Sherratt, Andrew, ed. *The Cambridge Encyclopedia of Archaeology.* New York: Crown Publishers, 1980.

Sickman, Laurence and Alexander Soper. *The Art and Architecture of China.* Baltimore: Penguin Books, 1956, 1974.

THE HEART OF THE GODDESS

Sieber, Roy, and Roslyn Adele Walker. *African Art in the Cycle of Life*. Washington, DC and London: Smithsonian Institution Press, 1987.

Singh, Madanjeet. *Himalayan Art*. New York: The Macmillan Co., 1968.

Sjöö, Monica. Personal Interview. Pt. Reyes, CA, 1988.

*Sjöö, Monica, and Barbara Mor. *The Great Cosmic Mother*. San Francisco: Harper & Row, 1987.

Smithsonian Institution (1). *Celebration: A World of Art & Ritual*. Washington, DC: Smithsonian Institution Press, 1982.

--- (2). *Aditi, The Living Arts of India*. Washington, DC: Smithsonian Institution Press, 1985.

Snow, Dean. *The Archaeology of North America*. London: Thames and Hudson, 1976.

**Spretnak, Charlene (1). *Lost Goddesses of Early Greece: A Collection of Pre-Hellenic Mythology*. Boston: Beacon Press, 1978.

--- (2), ed. *The Politics of Women's Spirituality*. Garden City, NY: Anchor Press, 1982.

--- (3). *The Spiritual Dimension of Green Politics*. Santa Fe, NM: Bear & Company, 1986.

Sproul, Barbara C. *Primal Myths: Creating the World*. San Francisco: Harper & Row, 1979.

Starhawk (1). *Dreaming the Dark*. Boston: Beacon Press, 1982.

--- (2). *The Spiral Dance*. San Francisco: Harper & Row, 1979.

--- (3). *Truth or Dare*. San Francisco: Harper & Row, 1987.

*Stone, Merlin (1). *Ancient Mirrors of Womanhood*. Boston: Beacon Press, 1979.

* --- (2). *When God Was a Woman*. New York: Harcourt Brace Jovanovich, 1976.

Sutherland, Joan Iten (1). Personal Interview. Pt. Reyes, CA, 1989.

--- (2). Unpublished translations and adaptations, 1989.

Swann, Wim. *Lost Cities of Asia*. New York: G.P. Putnam, 1966.

Tanner, Clara Lee. *Prehistoric Southwestern Craft Arts*. Tucson, AZ: University of Arizona Press, 1976.

Teish, Luisah. *Jambalaya: The Natural Woman's Book of Personal Charms & Practical Rituals*. San Francisco: Harper & Row, 1985.

Teish, Luisah, and Uzuri Amini. "Eye of the Vulture." *Woman of Power*, Winter, issue 8, 1988.

Thompson, Robert Farris. *African Art in Motion, Icon and Act*. Los Angeles: University of California Press, 1974.

Todd, Judith. Telephone Interview. University of California, Santa Cruz, 1989.

Todd, Judith, et al. "Hill Reclamation Rituals." *Lady-Unique-Inclination-of-the-Night*, Cycle 4, Autumn, 1979.

Turner, Kay, ed. *Lady-Unique-Inclination-of-the-Night* magazine. Sowing Circle Press, P.O. Box 803, New Brunswick, NJ 08903. All issues.

Tyler, Hamilton. *Pueblo Gods and Myths*. Norman, OK: University of Oklahoma Press, 1964.

Valadez, Susana; Huichol Center for Cultural Survival and Traditional Arts. Personal Interview. Oakland, CA, 1988.

Vequaud, Yves. *Women Painters of Mithila*. London: Thames and Hudson, 1977.

Villanueva, Alma Luz. *Life Span*. Austin, TX: Place of Herons Press, 1985.

Vogel, Karen. Personal communications, 1986–88.

Vogel, Susan, and Francine N'Diaye. *African Masterpieces*. New York: The Center for African Art and Harry N. Abrams, 1985.

Von Franz, Marie-Louise. *Creation Myths*. Zurich: Spring Publications, 1972.

Walker, Alice. *The Temple of My Familiar*. San Diego: Harcourt Brace Jovanovich, 1989.

Walker, Barbara G. *Woman's Encyclopedia of Myths and Secrets*. San Francisco: Harper & Row, 1988.

Walker, Roslyn Adele (1). *African Women/African Art*. New York: African-American Institute, 1976.

--- (2). Personal Interview. National Museum of African Art, Smithsonian Institution, Washington, DC, 1989.

Warner, Marina. *Alone of All Her Sex: The Myth and the Cult of the Virgin Mary*. New York: Vintage Books, 1976.

Warner, Rex. Foreword to *Encyclopedia of World Mythology*. New York: Galahad Books, 1975.

Warren, Henry Clark. *Buddhism in Translations*. New York: Atheneum, 1973.

Washbourn, Penelope. *Seasons of Woman*. San Francisco: Harper & Row, 1979.

Washburn, Dorothy K., ed. *Hopi Kachina: Spirit of Life*. San Francisco: California Academy of Sciences, 1980.

Wassing, Rene S. *African Art*. New York: Portland House, 1988.

Waters, Frank. *Book of the Hopi*. New York: Viking Press, 1963.

Weigle, Marta. *Spiders & Spinsters*. Albuquerque: University of New Mexico Press, 1982.

Westwood, Jennifer, ed. *The Atlas of Mysterious Places*. New York: Weidenfeld & Nicolson, 1987.

Williams, Lorraine Maffi, interviewed by Eugenia Macer-Story. "Coming Back Into the Circle." *Woman of Power*, issue 12, 1989.

Williams, Walter L. *The Spirit and the Flesh: Sexual Diversity in American Indian Culture*. Boston: Beacon Press, 1986.

Willson, Martin. *In Praise of Tara*. London: Wisdom Publications, 1986.

Wisdom Publications. "Tibetan Art Calendar." London: Wisdom Publications, 1988.

Wittig, Monique. *Les Guérillères*. New York: Avon Books, 1969.

Wolkstein, Diane and Samuel Kramer. *Inanna: Queen of Heaven and Earth*. New York: Harper & Row, 1983.

"Woman." *Parabola*. Vol. V, no. 4, Nov., 1980.

WomanSpirit magazine. 2000 King Mt. Trail, Wolf Creek, OR 97497, 1974–1984 (back issues available).

Wosien, Maria-Gabriele. *Sacred Dance, Encounter With the Gods*. New York: Avon Books, 1974.

Wright, Burton. *Hopi Kachinas*. Flagstaff, AZ: Northland Press, 1977.

Wyman, Leland C. *Blessing Way*. Fr. Bernard Haile, O.F.M., trans. Tucson, AZ: University of Arizona Press, 1970.

Wynne, Patrice. *The Womanspirit Sourcebook*. San Francisco: Harper & Row, 1988.

Yoshikawa, Itsuji. *Major Themes in Japanese Art*, vol. 1. Tokyo: New York Weatherhill/Heibonsha, 1976.

Zimmer, Heinrich. *The Art of Indian Asia*, vols. I, II, III. Joseph Campbell, ed. Princeton, NJ: Princeton Bollingen Series, 1955.

ART AND MUSIC

Originals or reproductions of some of the artwork and tapes of some of the music mentioned in this book can be ordered from the following sources:

Ancient Images of Women: Posters, Notecards and Bookmarks. Available from Swinging Bridges Visuals, P.O. Box 369, Dickson A.C.T., 2602 Australia.

Asungi. 3661 N. Campbell Avenue, Suite 108, Tucson, AZ 85719-1524.

Colbert, Joann Powell. *Goddess Note Cards*. Available from Sequoia Graphics, 4141 Ball Road #178, Cypress, CA 90630-3465.

The GAIA Catalog. Available from Gaia, 1400 Shattuck Avenue #9, Berkeley, CA 94709 for $2.

The Goddess Catalog: Museum Quality Replicas from Greece. Available from Rainbow Serpent Enterprises, 2 Stony Hill Lane, West Nyack, NY 10994.

Goddess Reproductions. Catalog available from StarRiver Productions, P.O. Box 6254, North Brunswick, NJ 08902.

Goshorn, Shan. 1637 South Delaware Avenue, Tulsa, OK 74104.

Guanyin poster. Available from San Francisco Zen Center Bookstore, 300 Page Street, San Francisco, CA 94102.

In Her Image. Goddess jewelry. Catalog available from Box 353, Pt. Reyes Station, CA 94956.

Martin, Marcelina. Brochure of cards and photographs available from P.O. Box 697, Point Reyes Station, CA 94956.

Murphy, Charlie. *Canticles of Light* (tape). Available from Out Front Music, P.O. Box 12188, Seattle, WA 98102. (206) 324-1519.

Oda, Mayumi. c/o Roberta English Gallery, 250 Sutter Street, San Francisco, CA 94108. (415) 291-9770. By appointment only.

Reclaiming Community. *Chants: Ritual Music* (tape). Available from Reclaiming Chants, P.O. Box 14404, San Francisco, CA 94114.

Thiel, Lisa Siri. (1) *Prayers for the Planet*, (2) *Songs of the Spirit* and (3) *Tools for Transformation* (tapes). Available from Sacred Dream Productions, 6336 North Oracle Road, Suite 326-307, Tucson, AZ 85704.

Vogel, Karen, and Vicki Noble. *The Motherpeace Round Tarot Deck*. Stamford, CT: U.S. Games Systems.

Williams, Anne. "Song of the Jaguar". Tape catalog available from Earthsong Productions, P.O. Box 780, Sedona, AZ 86336.

The following images have been reprinted with permission:

XV The Goddess of Democracy. Photo by Tsao Hsingyuan.

XVI Precolumbian priestess. *Prehispanic Mexican Art* by Paul Westheim. Plate 44. Putnam, New York, 1972.

XVIII Sarvabuddha Dakini. Photo courtesy of Ajit Mookerjee. Nepal.

XX Goddess with Skybar. Photo courtesy of Peter T. Furst. Private Collection.

XXIV Prajnaparamita. Courtesy of Andy Weber.

2 Ceramic Vessel. Photo courtesy of the Museum für Volkerkunde, Berlin.

3 God Giving Birth. Courtesy of Monica Sjöö.

5 top The Great Goddess of Willendorf. Photo courtesy of the Naturhistorisches Museum, Vienna.

5 bottom Snake winding across double-eggs enveloped in flowing water: painted compositions on late Cucuteni dishes from Tomashevka, western Ukraine. c. mid-fourth millennium b.c. Courtesy of Marija Gimbutas.

7 The Great Goddess of Laussel. Photo by Jean Vertut. Courtesy of Mme. Yvonne Vertut, Musée d'Aquitaine, France.

9 The Bird-Headed Snake Goddess. Photo courtesy of The British Museum, Department of Egyptian Antiquities, London.

11 Ixchel the Weaver. Photo courtesy of Peter T. Furst. Museo Nacional de Antropología, Mexico.

13 Spider the Creatrix. Photo courtesy of the Oklahoma Museum of Natural History, University of Oklahoma, Norman.

15 Akua'ba. Ghana, Ashanti tribe, fertility fetish. Wood and string beads, height 26.2 cm., Gift of Gwendolyn Miller and Herbert Baker, 1963. 850.

Photo courtesy © 1989 The Art Institute of Chicago. All rights reserved.

17 top All Mother. Photo by Robert Edwards. Courtesy of the International Cultural Corporation of Australia, Sydney.

17 bottom Djanggawo Sisters. Courtesy of the Art Gallery of New South Wales and the Aboriginal Artists Agency Limited.

19 Tlazolteotl. Photo courtesy of Dumbarton Oaks Research Library and Collections, Washington, D.C.

21 The Birth Goddess of Catal Huyuk. Photo by Arlette Mellaart.

23 Gwandusu. Photo courtesy of The Metropolitan Museum of Art, New York.

25 Breast Bowl. Photo courtesy of the Department of Library Services, American Museum of Natural History. Neg. #334999. New York.

27 Diana of Ephesus. Photo courtesy of the Museo Archeologico Nazionale, Naples.

29 The Woodlands Nursing Mother. Photo by Dirk Bakker. Courtesy of the St. Louis Science Center 8X65 and the Detroit Institute of Arts WL23.

31 Amaterasu. Photo courtesy of the Board of Trustees of the Victoria and Albert Museum, London.

33 Mahuika. Courtesy of Robyn Kahukiwa.

35 Nut. Photo by the Archeologisches Institute, Cairo. *The Mythic Image* by Joseph Campbell. Plate 162. Princeton University Press. Bollingen Series C. Princeton, New Jersey, 1974.

37 top Queen Maya. Photo courtesy of The British Museum, Department of Oriental Antiquities, London.

37 bottom Tree Goddess. Photo by Eliot Elisofon. Courtesy of Life Magazine, © Time, Inc.

39 Hahai'i Wuhti. Photo courtesy of the Museum of Northern Arizona E5423, Flagstaff.

40–41 Mary, Mother of God. Photos courtesy of Giraudon/Art Resource, New York. Musée de Cluny, Paris.

43 La Virgen de Guadalupe. Courtesy of Ann Bario. Museo de la Basilica de Santa Maria de Guadalupe, Mexico.

45 Guanyin. Photo courtesy of The Nelson-Atkins Museum of Art, Kansas City, Missouri (Nelson Fund).

47 Tara. Photo courtesy of The Metropolitan Museum of Art, New York.

49 Isis Leading Queen Nofretari. Photo by Dr. Max Hirmer. Hirmer Verlag, Munich.

51 Ixchel and the Rabbit. Photo by Otis Imboden © 1975. Courtesy of the National Geographic Society, Washington, D.C.

53 Artemis. Photo courtesy of Giraudon/Art Resource, New York. Musée du Louvre, Paris.

55 Shalako Mana. Photo courtesy of the Museum of the American Indian. Heye Foundation, New York.

57 The Goddess of the Sea. West Baffin Eskimo Cooperative, Ltd. Cape Dorset, N.W.T., Canada.

59 Grandmother Growth. Photo courtesy of Peggy Hitchcock.

63 Dakini. Photo courtesy of the Asian Art Museum, The Avery Brundage Collection #B60 S502, San Francisco.

65 Winged Isis. Harvard University —MFA Expedition. Courtesy of the Museum of Fine Arts, Boston.

67 Aditi. Photo courtesy of Ajit Mookerjee. Andhra Pradesh, India.

69 Pele. Courtesy of Herb Kawainui Kane. Collection of Barry E. Moore.

71 The Motherpeace Death Card. Courtesy of Karen Vogel.

73 Persephone and Demeter. Photo courtesy of Alinari/Art Resource, New York. Eleusis Museum, Greece.

75 Inanna. Photo courtesy of The Oriental Institute of The University of Chicago.

77 Dzonokwa. Photo courtesy of The Department of Library Services American Museum of Natural History. Tr. #1956(2). New York.

79 Kali Ma. Photo by Max Maxwell. Courtesy of Ajit Mookerjee. Kangra. Himachal Pradesh, India.

81 Nut, Mother of Rebirth. Photos courtesy of The British Museum, Department of Egyptian Antiquities, London.

83 The Tomb Priestess. Photo courtesy of the Instituto Nacional de Antropología e Historia, Mexico.

85 Hine-titama. Courtesy of Robyn Kahukiwa.

87 Coatlique. *The Great Mother* by Erich Neumann. Plate 68. Princeton University Press. Bollingen Series XLVII. Princeton, New Jersey, 1955. Museo Nacional de Antropología.

89 Selket. Photo by Lee Boltin. Courtesy of the Lee Boltin Picture Library, Croton-on-Hudson.

91 Gabon Ancestor Mask. Photo courtesy of the Museum voor Volkenkunde, Rotterdam.

93 The Minoan Snake Priestess. Photo by Lee Boltin. Courtesy of the Lee Boltin Picture Library, Croton-on-Hudson.

95 The Cycladic Goddess. Photo courtesy of the North Carolina Museum of Art, Raleigh. Gift of Mr. and Mrs. Gordon Hanes.

97 The Chanting Priestess. *Master Works of Mexican Art.* Remojadas II, 300–800 c.e. L.A. County Museum Catalog #588. October, 1963–January, 1964. Los Angeles County Museum of Art. Collection: K. Stavenhagen, Mexico.

98 The Oracular Goddess. (Insert.) Courtesy of Marija Gimbutas.

99 The Oracular Goddess. Photo courtesy of the Musee National De Belgrade, Yugoslavia.

101 Bird-Woman. Photo by Ernest Mayer. Lukasi Uitanga. b. 1917. Povungnituk. "Bird-Woman," 1959. Black/green stone. 14.7 × 14.2 × 9.2 cm. Collection of the Winnipeg Art Gallery.

103 The Gelede Mask. Yoruba, S.W. Nigeria. Photo courtesy of the Musée Royal De L'Afrique Centrale, Tervuren. Belgium.

105 The Dreaming Goddess. Photo courtesy of the National Museum of Archaeology, Valletta, Malta.

109 Apsara. Photo by Wim Swaan. *Lost Cities of Asia.* Plate 77. G.P. Putnam's Sons, New York. 1966.

111 Circle of Women Dancing. Photo courtesy of The Ancient Art and Architecture Collection, London.

113 top The Cosmic Yoni. Photo courtesy of Ajit Mookerjee. South India.

113 bottom The Cosmic Yoni. Photo courtesy of Ajit Mookerjee. Bheraghat, Madhya Pradesh, India.

115 Yoni Rocks. Photo by Ken Hedges, San Diego Museum of Man.

117 Shakti. Photo courtesy of Ajit Mookerjee. South India.

120 top Adya-Shakti. Photo courtesy of Ajit Mookerjee. Alampur Museum. Archeological Survey of India.

120 left Heraldic Woman. Drawing by Jennifer Roberts. Original photo courtesy of the Museum of the American Indian, Heye Foundation, New York.

120 right Sheela-Na-Gig. Photo courtesy of the Royal Commission on the National Monuments Record, London.

121 top Manubi. Photo by Dr. John Stanton. Courtesy of the University of Western Australia.

121 left Ancestor Spirit. Photo courtesy of the Hamburgisches Museum für Völkerkunde, Hamburg.

121 right The Doorway. Photo courtesy of the Musée de L'Homme, Paris.

123 Green Gulch Green Tara. Courtesy of Mayumi Oda. Photo by Marcelina Martin.

125 Vajravarahi. Photo courtesy of the Werner Forman Archive, London.

127 The Goddess as Yogini. Photo courtesy of Ajit Mookerjee. National Museum, New Delhi.

129 Lilith. *The Great Mother* by Erich Neumann. Plate 126. Princeton University Press. Bollingen Series XLVII. Princeton, New Jersey. 1955.

131 Ishtar. Photo courtesy of Giraudon/Art Resource, New York. Musée du Louvre, Paris.

133 Aphrodite. Photo by Dr. Max Hirmer. Hirmer Verlag, Munich. Rhodes Museum.

135 bottom Xochiquetzal. Photo by Carmelo Guadagno. Courtesy of the Museum of the American Indian, Heye Foundaton, New York.

135 insert Smiling Remojadas. Photo by Peter T. Furst. Private collection.

137 Apsaras. Photos by Wim Swaan. *Lost Cities of Asia.* Plate 83. G.P. Putnam's Sons. New York. 1966.

139 The Horned Goddess. Photo by Henri Lhote. Courtesy of Mme. Irène Lhote.

141 Ochun. Courtesy of Asungi.

145 Gaia's Children. Photo © Marcelina Martin 1982.

147 Kannon with the Sword. Courtesy of Mayumi Oda. Photo by Marcelina Martin.

149 Grandmother Moon. "Honoring Full Moon," from the series, "Moontime: The Cycles of Life." Hand-tinted/hand-painted black and white photograph, 16 × 20. Copyright 1987 Shan Goshorn, Wolf-Clan Cherokee.

151 Ochumare. Courtesy of Asungi.

175 Author photo. Photo by Irene Young.

TEXT CREDITS

Grateful acknowledgment is made to the following for permission to reprint:

PART ONE: CREATION. For the quote from *The Birth Symbol in Traditional Women's Art* by Max Allen (Toronto: The Museum of Textiles, 1981), based on Merlin Stone's work in *Ancient Mirrors of Womanhood*, reprinted by permission of the author. The quote from *The Homeric Hymns* translated by Charles Boer, 2nd edition, revised (Dallas: Spring Publications, 1979), reprinted by permission of the author. The chants "We are an old people. . ." by Zsuzsanna E. Budapest, by permission of the author. The excerpt from the song "Mother of All Ages," copyright 1989 by Anne Williams, by permission of the author. The quotes from *The Sacred Hoop* by Paula Gunn Allen, copyright 1986 by Paula Gunn Allen, reprinted by permission of Beacon Press. The Mother Woyengi story, an extract adapted from *In the Beginning* by Helen Cherry and Kenneth McLeish, by permission of the publisher, Longman Group U.K. Ltd. The poems beginning "In the house with the tortoise chair" and "Oh, golden flower," copyright 1972 by Jerome Rothenberg, reprinted by permission of Sterling Lord Literistic, Inc. Translation and interpretation in conjunction with the original songmen, the material for All Mother and the Djanggawo Sisters from *Love Songs of Arnhem Land* by Ronald M. Berndt, by permission of the University of Chicago Press (Chicago: University of Chicago Press, 1976). The excerpt from "Womanwork," copyright by Paula Gunn Allen (Shadow Country, UCLA, Native American Poetry Series 1984), reprinted by permission of the author. The quote from *Blessingway* by Leland C. Wyman, copyright 1970, reprinted by permission of the University of Arizona Press. The quotes from *Wahine Toa* by Patricia Grace, reprinted by permission of Collins Publishers. The quote from *Book of the Hopi*, copyright by Frank Waters 1963, reprinted by permission of the author and Penguin Books U.S.A. The songs "Cornmother" and "Rainbow Woman," copyright 1984, from *Prayers for the Planet* by Lisa Thiel, reprinted by permission of the author. The quote from *Song of Sedna* by Robert D. San Souci (New York: Doubleday, 1981), reprinted by permission of the author.

PART TWO: TRANSFORMATION. The chant "It's the blood of the ancients. . ." by Ellen Klaver, with music by Charlie Murphy is from the recording *Canticles of*

Light, reprinted by permission of the author. The chant "She changes everything she touches. . ." from *The Spiral Dance: A Rebirth of the Ancient Religion of the Great Goddess* by Starhawk (San Francisco: Harper & Row, 1979, 1989), by permission of the author. The quote from *Pele and Hiiaka, A Myth from Hawaii* by Nathaniel B. Emerson, reprinted by permission of the publisher Charles E. Tuttle Co. The quote from *The Meaning of Aphrodite* by Paul Friedrich, copyright 1978 by the University of Chicago, reprinted by permission of The University of Chicago Press. "Inanna and the Divine Essences" by Enheduanna, from *Book of Women Poets from Antiquity to Now*, edited by Willis and Aliki Barnstone, copyright 1980 by Schocken Books Inc., reprinted by permission of Schocken Books, published by Pantheon Books, a division of Random House, Inc. The quotes from *Kali: The Feminine Force* by Ajit Mookerjee, copyright 1988, reprinted by permission of Destiny Books, a division of Inner Traditions International. "The Moon and the Year" from *In the Trail of the Wind* edited by John Bierhorst, copyright 1971 by John Bierhorst, reprinted by permission of Farrar, Straus and Giroux, Inc. The quote from the song by Charlie Murphy, from the recording *Canticles of Light*, reprinted by permission of the author. The quote from *Muntu, An Outline of the New African Culture* by Janheinz Jahn, copyright 1961, 1981 by Faber and Faber, used by permission. The quote from *Maria Sabina: Her Life & Chants* by Alvaro Estrada, translated by Henry Munn, reprinted by permission of Ross-Erickson Publishers (233 Via Sevilla, Santa Barbara, CA 93109, $16.95 Hdb plus $1.25 p & h).

PART THREE: CELEBRATION. The quote from *Tantra Asana* by Ajit Mookerjee, reprinted courtesy Ajit Mookerjee. The quote from "Eye of the Vulture" by Teish and Amini, reprinted by permission of Luisah Teish. The Chiricahua Apache girl's puberty rite songs collected by Morris E. Opler in 1933 at Mescalero, New Mexico appear in his book, *An Apache Life-Way*, reprinted by permission of the author. The "Homage to Tara," from *The Cult of Tara* by Stephan Beyer, reprinted by permission of University of California Press. The excerpt from a poem to Vajravarahi from a Tibetan text, from the Tibetan Art Calendar 1987, reprinted by permission of Wisdom Publications, Boston. The excerpt from a poem about Ishtar by Merlin Stone, author of *When God Was A Woman* (1976) and *Ancient Mirrors of Womanhood* (1979), by permission of the author.

Here are the names of organizations you can contact to help protect the rights of indigenous peoples and support the survival of the Earth herself. This is meant to be a representative sampling rather than a complete list, and I have focused on U.S. groups because of their accessibility. You might know of other, similar organizations you wish to support.

Give to them in your prayers and your actions—time, money and energy. The essence of the Goddess's teachings is that we are all interconnected. Please remember the peoples, cultures and places that have given us the beautiful art and myth collected in this book.

American Friends Service Committee
1501 Cherry Street
Philadelphia, Pennsylvania 19102
(215) 241-7000
AFSC's work is based on Quaker principles of peace, justice and respect for all people. Their programs include, for example, helping Salvadorean refugees in the U.S. build a better life, anti-apartheid educational and assistance programs in South Africa, a Legal Aid Center in East Jerusalem to inform Palestinians of their rights under Israeli law and developing economic alternatives for threatened nomads in Mali.

Arbofilia
The Basic Foundation
P.O. Box 47012
St. Petersburg, FL 33743
(813) 526-9562
Arbofilia is a non-profit Costa Rican Organization founded by Costa Ricans of limited economic resources. The organization's goal is to combine agriculture production with environmental restoration. Arbofilia is a humanitarian organization dedicated to the betterment of human lives through restoration and conservation. Arbofilia emphasizes the protection of the culture, dignity, and creative potential of the most needy groups within Costa Rican society. The work of Arbofilia concentrates on the most environmentally degraded and economically depressed areas within the country. They will plant a single tree for $5.00 or 1000 trees for $250.00 in Costa Rica.

Cultural Survival Incorporated
53A Church Street
Cambridge, Massachusetts 02138
(617) 495-2562
Since its formation in 1972, Cultural Survival has supported projects on five continents to help indigenous peoples survive, both physically and culturally, the changes brought by contact with expanding industrial society. Project evaluations, research and dissemination of research results serve to educate the public, influence development theory and policy and stimulate debate among academics, planners and indigenous people.

Defense for Children International
210 Forsyth Street
New York, New York 10002
(212) 353-0951
DCI says it is the world's only organization concerned exclusively with defending and advocating human rights for children. They investigate child abuse all over the world, represent children in national courts, public research, raise public consciousness about children's rights, create innovative support and advocacy programs for children and engage in political lobbying with national and international institutions.

Environmental Defense Fund
257 Park Avenue South
New York, New York 10010
(212) 505-2100
EDF brings together scientists, economists and attorneys to devise practical, economically sustainable solutions to a wide range of environmental problems, from the greenhouse effect and acid rain to the protection of wildlife and endangered species.

Friends of the Earth
218 D Street, S.E.
Washington, D.C. 20003
(202) 544-2600
FOE has recently merged with the Environmental Policy Institute and the Oceanic Society. Their combined goals are the preservation, restoration and rational use of the Earth's resources. Among their top priorities are tropical deforestation, the greenhouse effect, groundwater contamination and agricultural biotechnology. FOE has affiliate organization in 37 countries.

Global Fund for Women
750 North California Avenue, Room K-3
Palo Alto, California 94303
The Fund is a grant-making foundation that funds women's activities internationally in the areas of female human rights, communications and economic autonomy for women.

Greenpeace U.S.A.
1436 U Street, N.W.
Washington, D.C. 20009
(202) 462-1177
Greenpeace is an international environmental group
which focuses on direct action. They have been involved
in such projects as challenges to the whaling industry,
nuclear weapons and toxic waste dumping, and the
protection of Antarctica. They are affiliated with
Greenpeace Action, which promotes environmental
protection and disarmament through grassroots
organizing, education and legislation.

Huichol Center for Cultural Survival and Traditional Arts
P.O. Box 1430
Cottonwood, Arizona 86326
(602) 634-3946
Living in a remote mountain area of Mexico, the
Huichol people have maintained their culture largely
unchanged for over one thousand years. The Huichol
Center in Nayarit provides free meals, legal assistance,
shamanic and Western medicine and material support
and marketing (through the Arizona center) for traditional Huichol arts. As a result, many Huichol women
and men are now supporting their families by selling
their artwork instead of by working for low wages in
pesticide-covered tobacco fields.

International Defense and Aid Fund for
Southern Africa, Women's Committee
P.O. Box 17
Cambridge, Massachusetts 02238
The IDAF is a humanitarian organization that has
worked since 1952 for peaceful and constructive
responses to the problems created by racial oppression
in South Africa. The Women's Committee was formed
to organize a network among U.S. women for the support and assistance of Black women in Southern Africa.
They work through women's groups, churches and clubs
to assist women inside South Africa and Namibia, as
well as women in refugee camps.

Kali for Women
N84 Panchshila Park
New Delhi 110017, India
Kali for Women seeks to increase the body of knowledge
on women in the Third World. Equally the organization is concerned with ensuring that, as far as possible, Third World women be provided an opportunity
to speak for themselves, rather than have their situation represented by the West.

Katalysis
1331-A North Commerce Street
Stockton, California 95202
(209) 943-6165
This North/South development partnership agency
operates a Women's Village Bank Program, which works
with a local women's self-help organization in Honduras
to train groups of rural women to run their own
cooperative banks and start up small businesses. They
hope to expand their program throughout Central
America.

Native American Rights Fund
1506 Broadway
Boulder, Colorado 80302
(303) 447-8760
NARF is a national legal defense fund working directly
with Native Americans to promote self-determination
for Indian people. Its five priorities are the protection
of tribal existence; the protection of tribal resources;
the protection of Native American human rights and
basic freedoms, including religious freedom; the
accountability of the federal government to live up to
its responsibilities to Native people; and the development of Indian law.

Natural Resources Defense Council
40 West 20th Street
New York, New York 10011
(212) 727-2700
NRDC uses legal action to challenge corporate pollu-
tion, works to establish meaningful federal environmental programs and takes a leading role in shaping critical
environmental legislation.

Pacific Campaign to Disarm the Seas
c/o Peace Resource Center of San Diego
5717 Lindo Paseo
San Diego, California 92115
(619) 265-0730
The Pacific Campaign works to free the Pacific Basin
and its people from the twin threats of naval intervention
and nuclear war. As a network rather than a centralized
organization, the PCDS finds the resources and chan-
nels them to participating groups at the grassroots level.

Pele Defense Fund
P.O. Box 404
Volcano, Hawaii 96785
The Fund was created in response to plans for a giant
geothermal project on the slopes of Hawaii's Mauna Loa

volcano, which native Hawaiians consider sacred to the goddess Pele. In addition to filing legal challenges based on the religious rights of native peoples, the Fund is also educating people about the plan's environmental consequences, including development of the pristine Wao Kele O Puna rainforest.

People for the Ethical Treatment of Animals
P.O. Box 42516
Washington, D.C. 20015
(301) 770-7444
PETA is a national animal protection organization with more than 250,000 members dedicated to establishing the rights of animals. They work to put an end to the fur industry, laboratory experimentation and cosmetics testing on animals and other forms of cruelty and exploitation.

Rainforest Action Network
301 Broadway, Suite A
San Francisco, California 94133
(415) 398-4404
RAN works nationally and internationally to protect the world's tropical rainforests. They use direct action, such as letter-writing campaigns, product boycotts and demonstrations against corporations which contribute to the destruction of the rainforest.

Seva Foundation
8 North San Pedro Road
San Rafael, California 94903
(415) 492-1829
Seva, whose name is a Sanskrit word meaning "service," began with anti-blindness programs in India and Nepal. They now also work with Guatemalans, Guatemalan refugees and Native Americans on education and public health projects. In addition Seva has been involved in village development, reforestation, urban housing and homelessness relief.

Sierra Club
730 Polk Street
San Francisco, California 94109
(415) 776-2211
The Sierra Club is a grassroots organization, most of whose members are in the Western United States, which focuses on preservation of wilderness and protection of the environment. They educate the public through publications and work for pro-conservation legislation; local chapters organize outings and trips into wilderness areas.

Tibetan Nuns Project
P.O. Box 40542
San Francisco, California 94140
(415) 647-2585
Through slide shows and other presentations, it informs the American public and raises funds to help support literacy campaigns and construction projects benefiting Tibetan Buddhist nuns, who, unlike monks, receive virtually no aid from other funding sources.

U.S. Tibet Committee
241 East 32nd Street
New York, New York 10016
(212) 213-5011
A nationwide human rights organization concerned with Tibet, with a dozen regional branches all over the U.S., it is staffed by Tibetan and American volunteers.

Wilderness Society
1900 17th Street, N.W.
Washington, D.C. 20006
(202) 833-2300
The Society's activities are devoted exclusively to the preservation of wilderness and management of public lands and natural resources. Through lobbying, grassroots organizing and public organization, they work for the protection and enhancement of the national parks, forests, Bureau of Land Management land and wilderness systems.

Woman to Woman
5825 Telegraph Avenue
P.O. Box A
Oakland, California 94609
(415) 652-4400, ext. 419
This campaign supports AMES (Women's Association of El Salvador) and AMNLAE (Luisa Amanda Espinosa Women's Association, Nicaragua). Its goals are to inform other women about the situation of women in Central America and to raise funds to support the rebuilding of childcare centers destroyed by the Contras in Nicaragua, to build childcare centers in the liberated zones in El Salvador, and to care for refugee children in Managua, Nicaragua.

Women Strike for Peace
145 South 13 Street
Philadelphia, Pennsylvania 19107
Since 1961, WSP has worked to achieve international disarmament under effective controls; to ban nuclear testing; to end the arms race and abolish all weapons

of destruction; and to join with women throughout the world to challenge the right of any nation or groups of nations to hold the power of life or death over the world.

World Wildlife Fund
1250 - 24th Street, N.W.
Washington, D.C. 20037
(202) 293-4800
The largest international conservation organization in the world, WWF is in the forefront of the struggle to protect the world's threatened wildlife and the habitats they need to survive. WWF directs more than 500 scientifically based projects, including emergency rescue programs, conservation education and direct land acquisitions.

WorldWIDE: World Women in the Environment
1250 - 24th Street, N.W., 4th Floor
Washington, D.C. 20037
(202) 347-1514
WorldWIDE has four goals: To establish a worldwide network of women concerned about environmental protection; to educate the public and policy makers about the vital links between women, natural resources and sustainable development; to promote the inclusion of women and their environmental perceptions in the design and implementation of development policies; and to mobilize and support women, individually and in organizations, in environmental and natural resource projects and programs.

20/20 Vision
1181-C Solano Avenue
Albany, California 94706
(415) 654-7544, (800) DISARMS
Each member receives a monthly postcard spelling out the most important 20-minute action one can take that month to work for global security, which is defined as countering worldwide environmental threats and the arms race.

Photo by Irene Young.

Hallie Iglehart Austen's lifelong interest in Goddesses began when, at the age of twelve, she started studying ancient Greek language and mythology. After graduating from Brown University in literature and classics, she studied religion and mythology in Europe and Asia. This experience, described in her book Womanspirit, *led to her synthesis of feminism and spirituality. Since 1974, she has been leading Goddess workshops, rituals and conferences, including those at the University of California, United Nations Women's Conference and numerous other institutions throughout the country. Her* Heart of the Goddess *multi-media presentation combines art, music, poetry and dance in an experiential invocation of the Goddess. She also created* Womanspirit *meditation tapes with harpist Georgia Kelly.*

Hallie, who adopted her matrilineal surname, lives in the San Francisco Bay Area, where she leads workshops, retreats and year programs for those committed to healing themselves and the Earth.

Contact Information

For information on *The Heart of the Goddess* meditation
tapes, multi-media presentations and retreats,
send a self-addressed business size envelope
with stamps for two ounces, to:
Women in Spiritual Education (W.I.S.E.), P.O. Box 697,
Point Reyes Station, California 94956.